C000252945

VIBRATIONS
OF **LIFE**

A Handbook for
Energetic Wellbeing

Su Mason PhD and
Kathleen Judd

BALBOA.PRESS
A DIVISION OF HAY HOUSE

Balboa Press books may be ordered through booksellers or by contacting:

Balboa Press
A Division of Hay House
1663 Liberty Drive
Bloomington, IN 47403
www.balboapress.co.uk
UK TFN: 0800 0148647 (Toll Free inside the UK)
UK Local: 02036 956325 (+44 20 3695 6325 from outside the UK)

Print information available on the last page.

ISBN: 978-1-9822-8195-3 (sc)
ISBN: 978-1-9822-8196-0 (e)

Balboa Press rev. date: 10/01/2020

CONTENTS

ACKNOWLEDGEMENTS

The creation of this book has involved many people, to whom we are extremely grateful.

First and foremost, Gerald and Tom, our husbands and sounding boards, who also gave their support by generously allowing us to give so much time to our ventures.

Our gratitude also goes to the wider network of our families and friends, who have assisted in proof-reading and critiquing this work through several versions, from the first draft to the finished manuscript: Anna Mason, Dr Gerald Mason, Pete Beer, Yvonne Kirk and Lorraine Billings.

We recognise Patricia Bateman's immense contribution to the original *Omnes Healing* course notes on which this book is based. In addition, we thank Sally Chaffer who worked with Su Mason on the *Energ-eased* CDs and Anna Keeping who did the editing.

We also wish to convey our appreciation to those who have contributed their personal stories which are included as anonymous examples throughout this book.

Special thanks go to all our clients, *Omnes Healing* members and students (past and present), who unknowingly provided us with the impetus for writing this book because of their valuable feedback.

Last but by no means least, our endless gratitude goes to The Source of All That Is, for the much appreciated, unseen support and guidance in our lives.

INTRODUCTION

What's it all about?
What's the point?
Do I have a purpose and what is it?
How can I make my life better?

Have you ever tried to find the answers to such questions and been faced with a sea of information that either doesn't really resonate, or simply baffles you? If so, you may find this book helpful.

We know that for many people the religious route provides them with the answers and support they need. This book, rather than focusing on belief systems, addresses general spiritual principles.

By the word 'spiritual' we are referring to that aspect of the self which is not defined by only our mind or body - often known as our life force or soul – which is often overlooked and neglected in our lives.

Vibrations of Life explains that we are energetic beings in an energetic world and how to deal with the consequences of this as we live our lives.

Problems in life occur, but it is how we think

about and subsequently deal with these challenges which determines whether or not we can still have contentment.

The tools and techniques offered are tried and tested and WORK. If they are practised regularly, they help to raise and maintain the frequency of our energetic vibration, which is the key to creating a strong and balanced life force and positive wellbeing. The effects of a person's high energetic vibration ripple out positively into their life, influencing others, situations and their environment.

Whilst providing many examples, we have outlined basic spiritual principles and used them to explain and address the problems which people can encounter in everyday life. We have tried to link the various aspects discussed, because to fully understand one aspect, we often need to have knowledge of another.

We start with the rather big topic of who we really are, our reality and our purpose in life, as all the other aspects covered fit into this understanding. We also explore the concept of ourselves and the world being energy; share techniques to raise our energetic vibration (which is vital for wellbeing); examine the power of the mind and how we can use it to create a more positive life; discuss some useful spiritual tools to help ourselves and those around us and finally, we look at how these spiritual principles can help us with various life challenges.

Throughout, we have used the term 'Source' which is short for *The Source of All That Is/The Highest Source of Love, Peace, Joy and Healing/God/Allah/Universal Source/The Highest Vibrational Source, etcetera.* This gives the reader the option to substitute whatever works for them.

This book is a result of over seventy years of healing experience, teaching, channelling wisdom and guidance from Source and spiritual/personal development, which we have accumulated between us. We have had personal experience of how the concepts contained within are very helpful when coping with our own life challenges. As part of our spiritual work, we share our understandings with our clients and students and regularly receive feedback on how their lives have changed for the better as they gradually put these tools and techniques into practise.

The examples provided throughout the book are from a variety of people and are kept anonymous. Names have been changed.

We sincerely hope that you enjoy this book and that you find it a useful and practical guide to navigate your life journey.[1]

Su Mason PhD and Kathleen Judd

CHAPTER ONE

Who Am I?

What do you say when you meet someone for the first time, and they ask you about yourself? Most of us give a specific description of who we are based on our roles in life, what we do as employment, our position in our family (parent/grandparent/son/daughter/spouse), our characteristics, etc. We label ourselves in terms of what we see and experience.

Such descriptions cannot be who we really are though, because many of these aspects will change with time.

> *I was a teacher, but now I am a landscape gardener.*
> *I was overweight, now I am thin.*
> *I was married, now I am single.*
> *I was a teenager, now I am elderly.*
> *I was naïve but now I have become more cynical, etc.*

If such narratives about us change, then this implies that who we fundamentally are changes throughout our lives. Intuitively, this does not seem right because these fluctuating descriptions miss the core of who we truly are. Aspects of us may change but who we really are does not. So, who are we?

> Whenever I look in the mirror I see the face of a mature woman looking back at me! I don't feel like that woman. I feel much younger; that reflection I see in the mirror is not the real me.

Are We Our Thoughts?

We are thinking beings and spend much of our time doing this, our thoughts making us feel different emotions. So, do our thoughts and resultant emotions define who we are? They can certainly seem to, especially when we have habitual thought patterns.

> *I am a stupid old man.*
> *I am fat and ugly.*

Our thoughts and emotions change however, so they cannot comprise the constant description we are looking for.

> *I felt so proud of my promotion and happy at my increased wage, but worried that I might not be able to cope in my new managerial job.*

These explanations of ourselves as our external bodily roles and features, or our fluctuating thoughts and emotions, somehow miss the main essence of our being, don't they?

Defining Our Essence

Everyone has some degree of awareness and sensitivity to energy. We are not talking about physical energy, but the energy vibrations which make up our world. For example, have you ever walked into a room and felt you could cut the atmosphere with a knife and just known that an argument took place there? Or you may feel or know when someone behind you has entered your personal space, even if you can't see or hear them? Or you go to hospital to visit a friend, feeling fine before the visit, but afterwards you feel drained of energy?

The New Physics confirms that the world we live in is made up of energy vibrating at different intensities and frequencies. The chair you are probably sitting on is energy, so is your physical body. They are just vibrating at a lower frequency to, for example, thought energy and so appear as form or matter (McTaggart 2003).

> I just felt this person's anger as he approached me. He felt threatening and I wish I had listened to my feelings 'cos I'd have run away and not ended up being mugged.

3

We can feel energy because we are also an energy, a life force. This energy, within our physical body and expanding outwards, is called the Human Energy Field, or aura, and is an aspect of our emotional and spiritual being (Brennan 1988). It can be felt and seen by the naked eye (with practise) and photographed using Kirlian photography.

We are energetic beings living in an energetic world - an energy with a consciousness because we can think, reason and feel emotions.

We are energetic beings living in an energetic world

What Happens to This Energy When We Die?

Many people feel that when they die, their consciousness dies too, as it is bound to their body. However, it is difficult to accept that we simply cease to exist when we die. Are our personalities, thoughts, feelings and experiences really completely lost?

In physics, the *Law of Conservation of Energy* states that the total energy of an isolated system remains constant. Einstein explained that this means that energy cannot be created or destroyed; it can only be transformed from one form to another. If we are an energy field, then Einstein's *Law of Conservation of Energy* also applies to us. We can transform into different types of energy, but we cannot be destroyed. The *Law of Conservation of Energy*, therefore, supports the idea that we do not cease to be when we die, but rather we transform.

Mediums can contact the conscious energy of those who have died and deliver messages from them to living relatives and friends (Smith 2018). Many people have had near-death experiences and describe the continuing of their awareness, even though their physical body has 'died' (Moorjani 2014; Olsen and Nelson 2012). Many testimonies exist from ordinary people who assert that they have experienced various phenomena, convincing them that life continues in a different form after the physical body dies (Cheung 2013).

> The first time I had a direct experience of the continuing of the soul after death was when I was a student nurse. It was at night and I was in the middle of laying out a patient who had just died, soon after being admitted to hospital. As I was about to shut his eyes, I very strongly felt his presence above and behind my left shoulder. I was in no doubt at all that this presence was the man who had just died, even though I had no prior experience of anything like this. In my mind I spoke to him and told him that I would be careful with his eyes. It just seemed like the polite thing to do! I was just amazed by his presence outside of his body.

Here is another example:

> I just know that Savita is still here. I feel her around and I know that she is looking after us (Mother of daughter who has died).

This could not happen if the energy of our consciousness was to end when we die. We appear to have a continuing inner dimension.

Connectedness

The fact that we are energetic beings is why we often feel connected to other people, animals and nature. We talk about 'being on the same wavelength' or 'in sync' with someone.

This connectedness is not only at a worldly level. If we still our mind (through meditation or deep prayer, for example) we can connect to an unlimited, highest vibrational power, the Universal Source of Light, Love and Peace. When we do make this connection, which is something people from all cultures can and regularly do, it can be described as having a sense of Being or Beingness. We feel right, peaceful, still, we feel at home because we are linked to the power in the Universe, which is the Source of everything, including ourselves.

We can only experience a sense of Beingness when our mind is still and we focus on the present moment, for example, in meditation; then, not intellectually, but with experience, we really understand our connectedness to the *Source of All That Is* and appreciate who we are. We can understand and feel that we are part of something limitless and, as a part, so we are unlimited. We become aware of our true nature as energetic Beings and our connection to all things.

> Occasionally I sit in nature and I allow myself the freedom of attuning to Source for no reason other than the total peace and upliftment that attunement brings me. After a few moments I can sense my energies melding into those of the trees, the grass, the flowers, the water – even those of a human or animal companion beside me. Indeed everything, including me, seems to 'hum' at the same frequency and I feel totally connected to all that is. These moments seem 'timeless' and I return to physical life feeling rejuvenated.

Who or What is Source?

'Source' is the highest vibration of Universal Energy and is known by other names, such as 'Source of All That Is', God, Jehovah, Allah, etc.

Source might be considered to be Unconditional Love, the eternal, ever-present life force that exists in all forms of life (including us), not existing in time, with no beginning and no end.

The truth is that we are not simply a physical body who is able to think and feel, we are so much more. At our essence we are eternal, interconnected, unlimited beings. We are, and everyone is, part of All That Is.

7

Indeed, there is general agreement among religious philosophers, spiritual leaders and mystics that our soul (the energy of our consciousness) is the immortal essence of our Being, our true eternal self, an aspect of Source.

One of us received the following channelled[2] information from Source, giving further clarification:

> *We would like to tell you more about who you really are.*
>
> *You are not your body, nor your mind, nor a separate soul.*
>
> *You are all part of the Highest Vibrational Source, which some call God.*
>
> *You are all connected.*
>
> *You are all One.*
>
> *This you know in theory, but you do not apply in practise.*
>
> *In practise this means looking beyond the physical appearance of things.*
>
> *Beyond your apparent world and into the realm of connected feeling.*
>
> *To connect with All That Is, you need to quieten your mind, to find the still space within, that aspect of you which is of Source.*
>
> *Feel the vibration of this Source energy.*
>
> *Allow it to expand in your awareness and reach outwards*
>
> *In so doing you connect with your unlimitedness and become One with All That Is.*

Then hold on to this serenity.
Let the flow of this high vibrational energy be your guide and succour.
Allow the connectedness to All, to further expand your awareness and thus enable the unlimitedness of your true self to be realised.

Many people recount having connected to Source. For example, healers describe having feelings of profound, unconditional love and peace when attuned to Source during healing. Others describe this in deep meditation and some people tell of the unconditional love of Source experienced during a Near Death Experience (NDE).

Anita Moorjani (2014) recounts how she was rushed to hospital with end stage cancer, her organs had started to shut down and her family thought that she had died. She experienced a 'near death experience' where she had heightened awareness in an expanded realm and felt encompassed by unconditional love and sensed that she was 'home'. She felt connected to everything and that she was in a state where time and space are one. (Soon afterwards she made a complete recovery).

A Healer's Experience of Source:

> I had a direct and amazing 'empathetic near–death experience' of Source when I was sending distant healing one day.[3]

My experience took place in our living room when I sat down, on my own, to send distant healing to a gentleman I knew well and whom I knew was dying. As I attuned, I felt very strongly that he was scared, so telepathically I asked him if he would like me to accompany him – I don't know why I did that. To be honest, it now seems like rather a stupid thing to say. However, in my mind he answered that he would like me to do this.

Immediately, we were both transported in front of a central, white, golden Light, which further out was orange, then light red and darker red on the very outside. The gentleman was in front and to the right of me.

The main impression on me, however, was the extraordinarily powerful sensation of deep Peace and Unconditional Love emanating from this Light, which felt as though it filled up us both completely. We stayed there, bathed in this Light and then suddenly I was back in my living room, feeling overawed and a little shaken by the experience.

The gentleman died a few hours later and I like to think that he did so without fear after this experience.

For me, in the short-term, I felt very sad; not for the death of the gentleman for whom death was an end to his bodily suffering, but because I wanted to return to that beautiful place. That Light felt like home and despite the fact that I had young children and a husband whom I loved very much, I felt that the physical realm did not matter – and it shook me that I could feel this way.

This deep sadness lasted only a couple of days. Now I realise that the reason for this feeling was that I had made a short visit near to my real home in the soul world, reminding me of who I really am – of spirit – and that this earthly life is but temporary clothing.

These examples seem to confirm that our consciousness continues after our body dies.

So, Who Am I?

Abraham (described as the non-physical collective consciousness which speaks through Esther Hicks) states (Hicks, 2004, p16):

> *'You and that which you call Source are the same. You cannot be separated from Source. Source is never separated from you.'*

Quite amazingly, who we really are is an aspect of Source, this highest vibrational energy of Unconditional Love to which we can feel our connectedness at certain times, for example whilst meditating, during certain visualisations or praying.

If Source is Unconditional Love, (and that is certainly what it feels like when we connect with this wondrous highest vibrational energy), then our true reality is that we are also Unconditional Love. We seek Love in life because fundamentally that is who we are.

> *Love, which created me, is what I am.*
> A Course in Miracles Workbook, Lesson 229

Each one of us is an individualisation of Source energy in human form. We are eternal, energetic beings of Love connected to all. How magnificent!

Alan Watts, the philosopher (1915 to 1973) stated:

> *'Jesus Christ knew he was God. So wake up and find out eventually who you really are. In our culture, of course, they'll say you're crazy and you're blasphemous. ...However if you wake up in India and tell your friends and relations, 'My goodness, I've just discovered that I'm God,' they'll laugh and say, 'Oh, congratulations, at last you found out.'*

At our essence we are eternal, inter-connected, unlimited beings. We are aspects of Source who is Unconditional Love

Imagining the human form as a finger, if you look at the individual fingers on a hand, they look separate. When you look further up, you see that they are connected by the palm and linked by an arm and are part of the whole. Using this analogy, although we appear to be separate, we are actually connected to Source and also to each other, the individual fingers being part of the whole.

Summary and Implications

We are energetic beings – Recognising that we are energetic beings in an energetic world explains why we can feel the energies of others and 'pick up' energies which do not rightfully belong to us. It has implications for our health and wellbeing and highlights a need to manage our personal energy fields. (This is explained further in Chapter Three).

We are eternal – This realisation is a big help. It can allow us to 'see the big picture' and re-frame our problems if we understand that the issues we are currently experiencing are actually a very small part of our totality. (See Chapter Six for a discussion on further implications of being an eternal soul).

We are part of Source who is Unconditional Love – We are not small, individual beings. We are individualisations of Source energy in human form.

Firstly, being consciously aware of this allows us to realise our true magnificence, even when in physical situations where we feel small. When we consciously accept that we are really energetic beings and part of an Unconditionally Loving Source, it helps us to see beyond our apparent difficulties and feelings of inadequacy in our physical world. Thoughts create emotions, so bringing our awareness to our true magnificence helps to dissolve any worldly feelings of impotence and melancholy.

Secondly, the realisation that this is the true magnificence of ALL people and animals is incredibly useful when confronted by those who seem mean and unpleasant. They are almost certainly acting from an outlook of the physical world with all its apparent problems and inconveniences. If, however, you can look beyond the outer physical appearance of the person and their behaviour and see them as the soul they truly are (their energy of Unconditional Love) it helps to foster harmony and defuse situations. Your regard for them becomes highly vibrational and their demeanour changes positively. This is the true secret of harmonious relationships – regarding each other as the loving souls that we are, allows apparent discord on the physical level to dissolve and become unimportant.

Thirdly, living as connected beings of Unconditional Love means that we are never truly alone. We only need to reach out in stillness and energetically link to our Source of Unconditional Love, allowing this energy to fill our being, our soul, nurturing and reassuring us. (See the Appendix, Section C, for an exercise on how to do this.)

CHAPTER TWO

The Purpose of Life

'What's the point?' This is a common cry of many, especially young adults as they try to find their way in the world.

Many people merely exist, becoming bogged down with earning a living, duty, everyday tasks or just trying to stay alive. This way of living can become dry, burdensome and depressing. People tend to feel better if they have a definite purpose in life so that they can avoid feelings of unfulfillment. But how do they find that? What is our purpose?

Maybe our purpose doesn't have to be a grand thing. We don't have to become a Prime Minister, a President, a doctor, or successful in the business world. If we are energetic, eternal beings who are extensions of Source and create our earthly experience, perhaps our purpose is just to do that – to create and experience life. Maybe nothing more is needed. We come into life with various talents and enthusiasms for different things and it might be that our purpose is to express those talents and what we are passionate about – whether it be physical agility finding expression in dance or sport, a curious mind in academic research, a head for numbers or business or a talent for bringing joy or calmness to people.

> *'The meaning of life is just to be alive. It is so plain and so obvious and so simple. And yet, everybody rushes around in a great panic as if it were necessary to achieve something beyond themselves.'*
> Alan Wilson Watts

Our purpose may be nothing more than to live our earthly reality, expanding and creating it and thus allowing the energy of creation (Source energy/ All That Is/God) to expand – a bit like dancing for the love of dancing, simply being here without needing to justify our existence on a physical level. However, this viewpoint does not quite fully answer the question of our purpose in life. What about people who would love to express their talents but who, due say to financial constraints, are not able to do so? It can be argued that this is a current limit to their creation (more about that in Chapter Five). A step nearer to finding our purpose could be less about what we DO and more about how we ARE.

How Should we BE in the Reality we Create?

If we realise who we truly are, namely eternal, spiritual beings who are extensions of the highest vibrational energy of Universal Source, this changes everything. Making the conscious choice to act with Love and Be Love, expressing ourselves as our true reality and knowing that our acts of love will reverberate out, touching all, is to create and experience our lives positively. It allows the Loving energy of creation (Source/All That Is/God) to manifest through our own True Self.

Expanding on this, there is a positive channelled message which we received:

> *LOVE in any life positively alters all lives (your own and those of others) ... Thus, a decision to love will positively influence all, bringing heaven to Earth.*

Cohen (2015, p75) similarly writes:

> *The only question worth asking about any act is, 'Does this bring more joy into the world, or does it diminish joy in the world?' Here you have the simplest yet the most effective guide to all life choices.*

He later is more specific and says that our assignment on this Earth is where we are. It means that we don't have to be in grand positions to effect positive change. Where we are now is exactly right for our purpose of Being Love.

When we start out on a spiritual path, many of us have the idea that we are going to become different from who we are now. We search the internet, read books about spirituality, attend workshops and courses, hoping to find the magic formula for inner peace and contentment. Often it takes a while, after much frustration, to realise that in fact there is nothing outside of ourselves which is going to help. All we need to do is to look inwards. It is more about letting go than searching for more. When we look inwards and accept what we see; when we allow our BEING not our DOING to define us; when we recognise who we truly are, of Source and of Love, we find our true spiritual reality – and what a joy it is when this starts permeating into our lives!

Summary and Implications

We are extensions of Source; energetic, eternal beings who create and experience life.

How we should be whilst we do this? Being consciously aware of the fact that we are extensions of the Unconditional Love that is Source Energy automatically gives our existence a purpose – one of being in harmony with our true selves and manifesting Love in our lives.

Living a life of Love wherever we are and whatever we are doing, whilst we create and experience life, is our true purpose.

CHAPTER THREE

Positively Managing Our Personal Energy Field

Learning to manage our personal energy field can make a big difference to our health and how we experience life.

Transfer of Energy

We are energetic beings living in an energetic world. Energy moves and can be transferred, so we can acquire energies from other people and situations and vice versa.

Energy of a high vibrational frequency is what we call 'positive' energy whereas 'negative' energy is of a low vibrational frequency (Dispenza 2017).

Many people regularly find themselves feeling mentally and physically exhausted by the end of the day. This is particularly true for therapists, health professionals, social workers, teachers and the many other people who work in a caring capacity, or those who work in a service industry. What they are doing is unconsciously giving their own energy to people who are needy of positive, high vibrational energy, and they allow themselves to be drained by these people who have lower vibrational energies (who are, for example, angry, fearful or jealous, etc.). Their high vibrational, positive energy moves to balance out the lower vibrational or negative energy of others.

Energy transfer can work the other way too. We feel better and more energised when we are with joyous, peaceful and loving people. This is because, literally, our own energies are being topped up with their higher vibrational energy.[4]

What Happens if Our Human Energy Field has a Low Vibration?

There are some consequences of allowing our vibrational frequency to become low:

Firstly, we can become ill because a high vibrational frequency protects against illness (which is of a lower vibration).

Secondly, we are at risk of lower vibrational energy from other people entering our own energy field – because we are on the same low vibrational frequency level as them.

You may become aware of this happening, thinking '*What's got into me?*' For example, when standing in the supermarket queue you may suddenly start to feel angry and think, '*Why am I angry? I have nothing to be angry about at the moment.*' It doesn't feel like your anger - because it isn't. You have gained that lower vibrational energy of anger from someone else in the queue as it has entered your energy field.

Thirdly, if we are allowing our vibrational frequency to become low, we will not be able to function at our highest level.

BUT DON'T WORRY!

Energy transfer happens to 100% of people. It is part of what happens as we live as energetic beings in this energetic world and, we can do something about it.

How Do We Manage Our Energy Field?

The aim of managing our energy field is very simply **to raise the frequency of our energetic vibrations as much as possible.** When we do this, it acts as a protection, as lower frequency energies are not on the same vibrational plane. So, even if someone with a low vibration is in the same physical space as you, they cannot affect you, as they are not of the same frequency level.

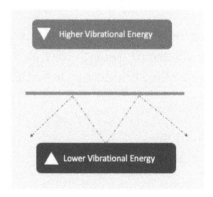

You may ask: '*If people with a low vibration can drain me, then even if my energy frequency is high, can I still be drained?*' The answer to that is '*No. Not if your vibrational frequency is **maintained** at a high level*'. So, if you feel that your energetic frequency is starting to dip, you will remain protected if you immediately do something to raise it again.

> Our aim in managing our energy field is to keep the frequency of our vibration high and protected and do something about it if we feel it start to dip

How Can I Raise My Energy Vibrations?

There are many different ways for people to raise their energy vibrations, though they may not realise this is the reason they find certain activities enjoyable, for example:

- Meditating
- Walking in nature

- Exercising - Stretching, shaking, bouncing can all release 'stuck' energy
- Being with joyful, loving people
- Gardening for pleasure
- Being in the present moment – this frees us at that moment from worrying about the future or having regrets about the past
- Spending time with animals
- Using visualisations
- Positive affirmations
- Receiving energy rebalancing from a high vibrational healer
- Avoiding negative people and situations

The trick is to DO things which make us feel happier and/or better.

High vibrations attract high vibrational people and situations

We should not feel guilty about nurturing ourselves because self-care raises our vibrations and is vital to our wellbeing. Indeed, if more people took the time to self-care, the world would be a happier place. High vibrations attract high vibrational people and situations. If you maintain your energy field at a high level, you are likely to find that your life takes a turn for the better.

Techniques to Raise Our Energetic Vibrations

The previously mentioned methods of raising our vibrations are not always things we can do on the spur of the moment, for example if we are at work or in a crowded place. So, it is useful to know about visualisation exercises which are very practical tools to self-manage our energy fields.

How do Visualisation Exercises Work?

A visualisation is not just day-dreaming or idle imaginings. It is the use of our thoughts to influence and create in our lives; to help us become how we want to be.

The reason for this is because everything is energy, including our thoughts, and energy has power to effect change. So, our thoughts have the power to result in change.

Studies of the brain, using functional MRI scans, have demonstrated that similar areas of the brain are activated whether we perform an action ourselves, read about it, or watch someone else do it...which is why action movies are exciting and horror films so scary. It is also why visualisation works.

If you don't believe us, try this short visualisation:

Feel your feet on the floor. Close your eyes and imagine that you are walking towards a fridge. Open the door and take out a large, bright yellow, juicy lemon. Shut the fridge door and place the lemon on a chopping board. Taking a sharp knife, cut into the lemon and see the juice run off the flesh. You can smell the fresh, citrusy, lemon. Now, pick up half of the lemon and squeeze the juice onto your tongue...

Now feel your feet on the floor and open your eyes.

This short visualisation is likely to have caused you to produce saliva and for some people, it results in them also smelling a lemony aroma. So, by imagining that lemon juice was being squeezed onto your tongue you stimulated the same region of the brain that would have been activated if you had actually tasted the juice. Just the thought of the lemon has the power to produce a very real physical response.

Thoughts have power. The thoughts produced in visualisations have

power to produce a real physical response

Visualisation Exercises

Please see the Appendix for three different visualisation exercises[5] which are specifically designed to raise the frequency of our energetic vibrations. In different ways, each aims to bring high vibrational energy into our being. Have a go at each and then, taking into account how long each one takes, choose the one that best suits your situation throughout the day.

A. **The Breathing in Peace Exercise** - This is the simplest exercise and is a really useful tool to help you de-stress. It can be done anytime, anywhere and is one way to quickly transform your personal energy from negative to positive. You can do it subtly. People with you need not know that you are doing it.

B. **Sun Visualisation Exercise** - This is a quick and easy way to raise your energetic vibrations and can be used regularly, throughout the day. Children usually find it easy to do this exercise.

C. **Source Connection Visualisation Exercise** - This is a very powerful visualisation. There are two versions of this exercise to raise your vibrational frequency by connecting with the Universal Source of Light, Love and Peace. It is great to do before you get out of bed or first thing in the morning, so that you start off the day as highly vibrational as possible. This visualisation exercise is one we strongly recommend to our clients and all our healer students to help them self-manage their energy field. So many people have told us the positive difference this exercise has made to their lives.

You might be interested to learn that the Sun and Source Connection Visualisation Exercises were channelled to us specifically for this purpose.

Precautions About Visualisation Exercises

1. **Please follow the instructions.** Using visualisations regularly is a simple, but very powerful tool, to harness the power of your thoughts and the creativity of your mind. However, you need to do these correctly. For example, one lady was still feeling drained after doing the Source Connection Visualisation Exercise because she was bringing energy *through* herself not *to* herself. Or people can forget to ground themselves and so can feel spaced out afterwards. **We urge you to read through these exercises in the Appendix when you do them the first few times, so**

that you follow the suggested sequence, which is specifically designed to ensure energetic safety.

2. **Do not fall asleep doing them.** Please note, it is important that these exercises are not done whilst lying down in bed prior to sleeping, as you may fall asleep before bringing your energies back to an appropriate level and leave yourself energetically open. This could result in an energetic imbalance.

3. **Ground yourself afterwards.** You will notice that in the Appendix, the visualisation exercises start and finish with wording which encourages you to feel your feet on the ground and that if you are feeling 'spaced out' afterwards you are asked to do a further grounding exercise (Appendix, Section E).

This is because the visualisation exercises are intended to raise your energetic vibrations which may result in you feeling 'spaced out', especially if your baseline energy vibration level was low.

Much like how the earth wire in an electrical plug prevents us from getting an electric shock from any build-up of electrical charge, grounding helps make sure we don't become overloaded by a build-up of high vibrational energy, after energy exercises. In this sense, grounding our physical body is also a type of energy protection and is easy to do.

Practise Often for Energy Wellbeing

Visualisation exercises cannot work if you don't do them

These visualisations **cannot work if you don't do them** and they can all be done quite quickly.

It is a good idea to **do these exercises regularly** so that **your energetic vibration is regularly raised.** We suggest, at least first thing in the morning and before you go to bed at night, but also before any situation which you think might be difficult.

How to Construct Your Own Visualisation

Some people have specific issues in their life which they would like to work on. Making up your own visualisation is a useful way of addressing these and/ or if you do not resonate with any of the visualisation exercises in the Appendix.

There are three main points to note when constructing your own visualisation:

1. It should promote thinking in a way which **uses all your senses** to create a positive vision of how you would like things to be. Many people find it difficult to see pictures in their mind, but

you only need to sense or get a feeling for what you wish to create.

2. Please note that it is very important to use the **present tense**. If your thoughts are that you *want* to be happy, the energy of *wanting to be happy* is what you will create. But if you visualise, with thanks, that you ARE happy, then this positive thought energy helps create that reality.

3. It is also important **to only use positive sentences** in your visualisation. This is because the brain does not compute the negative word in a visualisation, and you might end up creating the opposite of what you want. For example, if someone says to you, '*Don't think of a pink elephant*' – What are you doing? You are probably thinking of and picturing a pink elephant! Your brain needs to first think of the elephant and then try to push it out of your mind to obey the 'Don't' thought. So instead of visualising: 'I am not tired or no longer tired', where the brain hears the word, 'tired' and this state is reinforced, it's better to think: 'I am full of energy' – the actual state that you want to create.

Affirmations to Use With Your Visualisation Exercise

An affirmation is a statement of intent to express how we want our lives to be. When you are making up your own visualisation it is very useful to include a high vibrational affirmation to emphasise how you would like to be. Here are some examples:

- I am a peaceful person
- I am content
- I shine out with unconditional love for myself and others
- I am growing stronger and stronger both mentally and physically

If you make up your own affirmation, you just need to remember to use the present tense and positive wording and use it regularly.

Practise Constructing Your Own Visualisation

Here is how to make up your own visualisation:

- To start, have your feet on the floor and feel the ground beneath you.
- Shut your eyes and take a few deep breaths to help you relax, then return to breathing normally.
- Think of the high vibrational wording you wish to use.
- Visualisations should construct a real feeling for the sense of what is being created. Include as much detail as possible: What do you look like? Where are you? What are you doing? Is anyone with you? What can you hear yourself

31

and others saying? Add as much detail to your image as you can to get a real feeling for the scene.

- Finally, bring your attention back into the room. Rub your hands on your thighs and feel your feet on the floor and when you feel ready, open your eyes.

If you are NOT FEELING FULLY GROUNDED or FEELING SPACED OUT after this visualisation, please see Section E at the end of the Appendix for further grounding exercises.

Results of Maintaining High Energetic Vibrations

It is really worth keeping the frequency of our energetic vibrations high because it has all the following benefits:

1. **Protects** us from lower vibrational energies transferring to our energy field, such as other people's anger or fear. Maintaining our energy frequencies at a high vibration is in fact the **most effective energy protection,** as lower vibrational energies are not at the same level and so cannot affect you.

2. **Helps maintain health** as lower vibrational disease is not on the same energetic plane. It is worth noting here, however, that illness is complex. There are many different causes. Highly

vibrational people can also become ill, (although they are less likely to than people who have low vibrational energy) and they are more likely deal with illness in a more philosophical way.

3. It is how our energy fields are meant to be and so **leads to harmony** in life, both within yourself and with other people.

4. **A person with a highly vibrational energy field can positively influence situations**. When they enter a room, often you can sense their positive energy and they can affect situations positively. So, by caring for ourselves and maintaining our energies at a high frequency, we can positively influence situations and our environment, such as our workplace or home.

Maintaining a high vibration is the most effective energy protection

Further Energetic Protection

Bubbles of Light Protective Visualisation (See Section D in the Appendix)

There are times when you might be feeling unwell, or not confident that your energy is vibrating highly enough to counteract negative emotions, such as great anger. Or you may be in a situation where you feel that your energy is liable to be drained by others. At these times, the Bubble of Light visualisation is a very useful and quick method of protecting your energies instantly.

Remember we explained that as thoughts are energy, they have power. In this visualisation, the intention is that you and the source of negativity, (whether it be a person or a situation) are separated in two individual bubbles of light. If you are separated through this visualised intention, then the negativity is also separated from you. Simple, but very effective.

For example, you can use this method to separate the television from you if you enter a room with a negative programme, such as a horror film, being broadcast. It works. You don't feel affected by the negativity with a bubble of light around you and another around the television.

Summary and Implications

Managing our energy field involves keeping the frequency of our energetic vibration high and protected and doing something about it if we feel it start to dip.

It is extremely important for our health that we take the time for ourselves to do something to raise our energetic vibrations regularly. It is not selfish, because managing our energy field not only creates a better reality for ourselves, it also positively impacts society and our lives. If everyone took the time to do this, our world would be a happier place.

CHAPTER FOUR

Our Reality

Chapter One asked the question 'Who Am I?' and offered various ways of defining our true self, with examples to help us become consciously aware that:

- we are not simply a physical body
- we can be thought of as being energetic, eternal, a part of and connected to Universal Source Energy/God/All That Is
- our reality seems to be that we are a spiritual being manifesting a physical body.

As Christian mystic Pierre Teilhard de Chardin said:

'We are not human beings having a spiritual experience; we are spiritual beings having a human experience.'

But what about our wider reality? What about our environment, the objects we see, our planet, the

Universe? If we are eternal, spiritual beings, what about all that we observe around us?

In this chapter we propose that our environment is also energetic. This can be a difficult concept to grasp as, frankly, much of our surroundings seem to be very solid. Please bear with us, however, as many of the New Physicists are also coming to this conclusion. We have not offered their detailed scientific explanations in this small book but have included a number of references in the bibliography section in case you would like to explore this further.

We are Linked to the Environment

It is widely accepted that our Universe is huge, with unbelievably large distances stretching between galaxies, but there are no voids. Time, mass, speed and distance are all intertwined within the quantum energetic fields which link everything to everything (Galfard 2016).

This seems to back up the Eastern philosophy contention that 'All is One'. We are not separate from our environment. The energy of who we are affects everything and we are affected by the energy around us. Dean Radin (2006) discusses this entangled fabric of reality. He writes that bioelectromagnetic fields around our bodies are entangled with electromagnetic fields in the local environment and with photons (energy) from the rest of the Universe.

I was acting as a guide to a group of twenty experienced meditators and had taken them to a sacred site in the UK. One area is housed inside a dark, stone built, enclosed, windowless construction, much like an old damp cellar. We had dressed the interior with a few tea lights, wildflowers and dishes of water.

Centrally there is a large 'healing pool' of still water, into which they all immersed themselves. A short while later, as they dried and dressed, the waters completely stilled again. In the space in front of the healing pool they then formed a circle, held hands and repeatedly chanted 'Ohm'.

As a newcomer to this kind of experience I was standing a short distance away from them, watching in amazement as the whole surface of the previously still waters of the healing pool rippled in response to the vibration from the repetitive 'Ohm' – even though we were in an enclosed space! At the side of the pool where I was standing there were large, thick, dining table sized slabs of sandstone, each dressed with our flowers, candles and dishes of water. I stepped forwards and put my whole hand palm down on the nearest stone slab. I was completely astonished to find that its whole surface was rippling under my hand, exactly like the surface of the pool! I snatched my hand away as I sensed a bolt of energy, like an electric shock!

As soon as the group had completed their chanting, I shouted in excitement,

'This huge stone just moved under my hand!'

'Well of course it did!' A member of the group replied (with an accompanying shrug of the shoulders). Still stunned by the experience, my response was, 'NO, NO, you don't understand – it *rippled*, the whole stone *rippled!'*

Another member of the group said, "But that's what happens."

'NO, NO,' I replied, 'this kind of thing doesn't happen to me!!'

"Well it does now!" they said in unison, and they both enveloped me in a hug.

This example seems to confirm that everything is energetically linked. The apparent stillness of the water and solidity of the stone changed in appearance to the human eye because they were perceived as liquid and solid matter, rather than energy that can change its vibration from one frequency to another. All the group members accepted that the vibrational frequency, the sound wave energy, of their meditational chanting had the power to influence the energy of the physical environment.

The Power of Personal Perception

R.C. Henry (2005), Professor of Physics and Astronomy at Johns Hopkins University, writes that physicists are acknowledging that the Universe is a 'mental' construction and that the observer creates the reality. As observers, we are personally involved with the creation of our own earthly reality.

> I had an appointment to get to. I had allowed what I imagined would be plenty of time for the journey, parking my car, then the short walk to my destination. En route, however, I was held up by slow moving traffic which meant that I would arrive late. Initially I panicked, aware that it would be many months before I would be offered another appointment – if at all, since I was about to miss this one. So, I decided to re-frame the situation and use a technique I had read about for 'stretching time'. With nothing to lose by doing this, despite its apparent weirdness, I simply decided to believe that if I think I don't have enough time, then that becomes my reality. So, I changed my thoughts to 'I am going to arrive in plenty of time for this appointment'. I continued my journey and purposely didn't look at the clock again until I had found a parking space. I was totally amazed to see that I had actually arrived a few minutes early and made it to my appointment after all!

Bishop George Berkeley, who died in 1753, defended two philosophical ideas: idealism (that everything that exists depends on a mind for its existence) and immaterialism (that things exist only when they are being perceived). He asked the hypothetical question which has teased many a philosopher, that if a tree falls in a forest and nobody is there to hear it, does it make a sound?

Michael Talbot asks:

> *'Is it true what the mystics had been saying for centuries – that reality is 'maya', an illusion; that reality is really a vast, resonating symphony of wave forms, a 'frequency domain' which is transformed into the world as we know it only after it enters our senses?'*

Pioneering physicist Sir James Jeans wrote:

> *'The stream of knowledge is heading toward a non-mechanical reality; the universe begins to look more like a great thought than like a great machine. Mind no longer appears to be an accidental intruder into the realm of matter, we ought rather hail it as the creator and governor of the realm of matter.'*

There are credible physics theories proposing that our thoughts influence and create events and physical matter

There are credible physics theories that are now proposing that our thoughts influence and create events and physical matter. The New Physics seems to explain the weird notion that our thoughts create our earthly reality and that everything is energetically connected. Some philosophers and many spiritual texts concur.

> *We are what we think, all that we are arises with our thoughts, with our thoughts we make the world.*
> Gautama Buddha

Similarly, Alan Cohen (2015; p106) clearly explains this viewpoint stated in the more modern 'A Course in Miracles':

> *The world is in you.*
> *Everything that seems to be in the world is in your mind.*
> *There is nothing outside of you.*
>
> *The body is a representation of mind and emotions...*
> *Your body doesn't cause your thoughts. It is a result of them.*
> (Cohen 2015, p101)

A Holographic Universe

A hologram is a three-dimensional image, created with photographic projection. The word is made from the Greek words holos (whole) and gramma (message).

There are claims that a possible explanation for the nature of reality is that it is holographic; that despite its apparent materiality, the Universe is actually a 3-D image projecting from a level of reality beyond time and space.

This idea was pioneered independently by physicist David Bohm and the neurophysiologist Karl Pribram. Bohm was a protégé of Einstein's and a respected quantum physicist. Both Bohm and Pribram independently arrived at their conclusions to make sense, not only of phenomena encountered in quantum physics and neurophysiological questions, but also paranormal and mystic experiences. This model is also being used by cosmologists to mathematically model the Universe.

Professor Kostas Skenderis (2017) at the University of Southampton is a mathematical scientist who considers that the entire Universe is a hologram. He explains, that, similar to an ordinary hologram (such as on a credit card) where a three-dimensional image is encoded in a two-dimensional surface, our physical environment which we can see, feel and hear (as well as our perception of time), emanates from a flat two-dimensional field where it is encoded.

The scientific hypothesis that the Universe is a

3-D image projecting from a level of reality beyond time and space seems incredible and, at the same time interesting from a spiritual point of view.

Acceptance that Source is a consciousness at a level of reality beyond time and space and, that we are aspects of Source, therefore indicates that *our* consciousness might be said to be projecting the Universe.

The Reality of the World

In one of our channelled messages from Source, we ask for explanations about our true reality. (The channelled message is in italics):

Please can you explain the reality of the world? If all is an illusion, as you say, then are you saying that Source did not create the beautiful aspects of the Universe and Earth, such as the wonder of a beautiful sunset over the ocean or the splendour of the mountains?

> *We have told you that your reality on Earth is an illusion. We have also told you that you are limitless facets of Source. If you put these two facts together you can see that humans, as creating facets of Source have created their current reality of the Earth in the Universe. Thus, you can conclude that as you are a facet of Source, Source via you, did create within the*

illusion. But only via you. The essence, which is Love, does not create, but just IS.

So, what about the bad aspects of the world?

Similarly, this is a creation of humankind, a facet of Source. However, it is important to remember that the essence of Source IS, and IS LOVE. It is through the connection of love that humankind does not become lost in the illusion forever. It is a temporary dream and therefore not reality.

So, you have to understand that your question does not really make sense as you are not really of the dream. It is but a temporary illusion and not your reality or that of Source of whom you are a part.

Source ensures that you are never lost in the dream. Your connection of love to Source is like a thread which links you always. Connect with love and you connect with Source.

The concept of our role in creating reality is expanded further by Source:

'If, as you have said, Divine Source is 'the centre and essence of all' then how come there is anger, hatred, fear, etc.?

There isn't.

Well it certainly seems that way when I look at the news.

> *This is because of how you view the world. You think of it as being where you are, don't you?*

Yes.

> *In fact, this is not the case. You only appear to be here. You only appear to be living in your body with others on this planet within this Universe. The reality is that you are with Divine Source, linked with Divine Source and all others whilst your collective Mind has moved outwards from this and thinks it is elsewhere.*

I have read about this, that we are collectively dreaming our lives, some of which are nightmares and some pleasant dreams. So, is this really the case?

> *Yes. The dreams you have at night reflect this reality and they do seem very real whilst you are dreaming them. To answer your earlier question, if you are projecting your collective mind outwards in this collective dream life, this represents only a projection (think of it like the projection of a film) of your mind and not really the Mind essence. So, the essence (or Source) is still with you, but not in the projection. It is difficult to explain in words to you, but the Divine Source of all is not the Source of the world, but*

you who are extensions of Source are projecting outwards and have formed this world through your collective, linked mind.

Why? Why are we not happy to stay with Divine Source?

You are created with free will. You simply willed the world.

So how can we have happy dreams or become aware that we have not left Source?

You have answered your question. Happy dreams can be had when it is realised that you are linked with Source and always have been. You never left. You are One with Divine Source.

Summary and Implications

Energetically everything is interconnected (All is One) – We are energy, connected energetically with everything. Therefore, the way we act, the quality of our thoughts and the energy we emanate affects our environment and all other beings. It helps us realise that we are not alone, and our thoughts and actions have wider influences than we may at first appreciate. Similarly, the reverse is true. We are affected by the energy around us, which, if negative, can have implications for our wellbeing. We discussed how to manage this in Chapter Three.

Theoretically, the Universe may be a 'mental' construction of our collective mind – This concept, although difficult to grasp or believe, does explain unusual occurrences, such as the rippling of the rock in the story recounted by one of our colleagues. The thought that we create our reality is extraordinarily powerful because it means that we can create a better one if we wish to do so. We shall talk about how to do this in Chapter Five.

It implies that anything is possible!

CHAPTER FIVE

Our Powerful, Creative Mind

In Chapter Four, we discussed that the New Physics, as well as many mystics and spiritual leaders, agree that our thoughts create our earthly reality and that everything is energetically connected. The Universe might be considered as a 'mental' construction and we, the observers, create the reality... so we can create a better one if we wish to do so.

Is this really true? If so, it is both an extremely empowering thought and also one that at first seems unlikely.

We see plenty of misery in the world. If people create their own reality, why would they knowingly create unhappiness?

How Do We Create Our Experiences?

Very simply, we create the experiences of our world through the energy of our thoughts. When we create something, we first create it in a thought form.

Nothing was ever made before someone thought about it first. Energy (which is everything) begins to flow through this thought form, energy of a similar vibrational frequency. Eventually, through repetition of this thought, it manifests on the physical plane as matter or a situation. This is what is known as the universal *Law of Attraction.*

Abraham, the non-physical collective consciousness which speaks through Esther Hicks (Hicks, 2004) states:

> *Your life, and everyone else's, too, is but a reflection of the predominance of your thoughts. There is no exception to this.*

This is not a new idea, it has been expressed by a variety of different people over the years, from Buddha, to Marcus Aurelius (Roman emperor from 161 to 180 AD and Stoic Philosopher) to Henry Ford (Founder of the Ford Motor Company).

The spiritual observation is that our outer space (our life) is but a reflection of our inner space (our mind). Our thoughts shape our destiny even if we are completely oblivious to this fact.

People don't deliberately create bad things in their life, however. Usually they are unaware that they are creating their own misery, generally blaming others and considering themselves as victims of fate. They simply do not realise that their thoughts and feelings are attracting low vibrational (or negative) stuff into their life. This is how we sabotage ourselves, blocking achievement of fulfilment and happiness in our lives.

We are energetic vibrational beings and we attract energy into our lives that is a vibrational match to our own

It's helpful to keep in mind the principles of the *Law of Attraction*: like energy attracts like energy and, as we are energetic vibrational beings, we attract energy that is a vibrational match to our own. So, if we feel stressed out, angry, resentful, fearful or sad, we are emitting negative energy, often attracting negativity into our lives in the form of the very experiences, people and situations that we are trying to avoid. On the other hand, when we have feelings of excitement, enthusiasm, joy, abundance etc., we are emitting positive energy and attract experiences, people and situations to match this.

My daughter was starting her second year at university and was moving into a flat above a kebab shop in the East End of London.

She and I drove down from Yorkshire with the back of the estate car filled to the brim with the many items she needed – a huge TV and stand, a suitcase of clothing, food provisions, a box of books and a flat-packed wardrobe and shelving.

'I'm really worried. We are not going to be able to park outside the flat. It is always busy and how are we going to lift this heavy stuff up the stairs? I don't want to ask just anyone to help 'cos I don't want them seeing in the flat', said Mia.

'It will be fine. I am visualising a parking spot right outside and someone lovely who will help us with the lifting', I replied.

My daughter rolled her eyes, 'I'm not saying that is not going to work, but it isn't going to work!'

'Just wait and see. I know it is going to be fine'.

When we finally arrived at the rundown kebab shop, we were able to park the car right outside. I grinned.

Mia was not mollified, 'So how are we going to get all this heavy stuff up into the flat?'

'Well let's start with carrying something which we can manage, like the stand for the TV'. (It was large but not very heavy).

As we lifted it out of the car, a man came over and asked if we needed any help.

'Well we're okay with this, but to be honest, I don't know how we are going to get all the rest of the heavy stuff up'.

'We'll help you' he said.

He and his work colleague had been doing some repair work in a nearby shop and they very kindly, moved all Mia's paraphernalia up the steep steps into the flat. We were delighted and afterwards offered them some money as a thank you. They refused to accept it!

Now Mia is a complete convert to the power of thought to create in our lives and says that she regularly tells her friends about it!

Every emotion we ever experience begins as a thought. It is not true that emotions happen to us. They are created by the thoughts we have. A situation, such as unexpected redundancy, can be viewed either negatively or as a positive opportunity and our emotions about this event are altered accordingly.

The only reason we don't have what we want in our lives is because we are not a vibrational match with what we desire. We can identify that this is the case when our emotions feel negative, indicating that we are in vibrational discord with how we would like life to be. In reality there is universal abundance available to us, but it can't come into our experience if we are not in vibrational alignment with receiving it. By releasing negative thought patterns, we raise our vibration and bring ourselves into alignment with receiving positive abundance. Abraham (Hicks 2004) explains that as energetic beings, we are vibrational transmitters broadcasting our signal at all times. To attract a better life, we need to change our broadcast. Vex King (2018) calls this the *Law of Vibration* as it explains WHY the *Law of Attraction* works.

How marvellous to realise that we have the power to change our reality for the better! The *Law of Attraction* is more than just 'positive thinking' however, and is not just about vague, wishful thinking about the future.

Experiments using biofeedback equipment demonstrate that every thought (energetic vibrations) affects every cell of our body and our human energy field. People can sense another's feelings through their aura. They do not have to be gifted psychics to do this. People often describe the energy fields of others and will say things like:

> He is prickly/down/low/cold
> She is radiant/warm/glowing

The upside of the creative power of our thoughts is that if we take control of them, we can take control of our lives for the better.

Bruce Lipton PhD, a cell biologist, was thrilled that he could change his life for the better by changing his beliefs. He liked that fact that there was a science-based way to change himself from being a continual victim to becoming the 'co-creator' of his destiny.

So, to Change my Life, All I Have to do is Think Positively?
...Sorry, Not Quite.

Bruce Lipton explains that it is not as easy as just saying that you are going to change your thought patterns and start to think positively. He writes that neuroscience divulges that the subconscious mind (an information processor, one million times more powerful than the conscious mind), is what actually controls our behaviour 95 to 99% of the time. This may seem surprising as most people think it is our conscious mind and thoughts that do this.

Sadly, this means that we only move towards our wishes and desires 1 to 5% of the day. In the remaining time, our lives are controlled by the habit-programmes downloaded into the subconscious mind which started during early childhood. The most fundamental of these programmes were downloaded by observing other people, such as our parents, siblings, teachers and community. Lipton says that the profound conclusion is that 95% or more of our lives has been programmed by others!

Additionally, since most of our behaviours are under the control of the subconscious mind, we rarely observe them, much less know that they are engaged. Not a comforting thought!

But I Want to Create Positive Experiences! How?

Firstly, we need to become aware of the correlation between our thoughts and feelings and what we are manifesting.

Since our emotional state indicates our vibrational frequency, an awareness of our emotions is a guide to the level of vibration we are emitting and therefore, what we are attracting into our lives.

> Our emotions are our guide to the level of vibration we are sending out and therefore what we are attracting into our lives

We need to take responsibility for our emotions (which are the result of our thoughts) and do something about changing them. This involves gradually changing our thought patterns to more positive ones, directly affecting our baseline emotions and thus guiding us to what we desire.

As Abraham (Hicks 2004) says, ... '*you may allow or you may resist Well-Being - but everything that happens to you is all your doing.*'

It's important that we make the effort to become fully aware of our thought patterns and belief systems, which may be limiting and negative and inhibiting the fullest expression of who we truly are. If we have been thinking negatively for years and have had negative programming of our sub-conscious mind since childhood, then it may seem difficult to deliberately change our thought patterns - but with real intention, it is possible to become more consciously aware, becoming the master of our thoughts rather than the slave to them. As Bruce Lipton bluntly states:

'No one is fixed until they make the effort to change.'

Learning the art of visualisation has transformed my life and removed me from consistently living on the edge of depression. I now own the belief that we are the creators of our reality, the good and the bad. In practising the art of visualising my desires and dreams, getting as clear as I could on details, I generated the feelings of positivity and excitement. As the momentum of clarity built, the Universe seemed to listen and doors opened, as if by magic!! How could I ignore the signs? I quit my corporate, well-paid job and walked into self-employment.

I manifested my own office and apartment. Within the first month, my bills were paid with food on the table. I know that I am being divinely guided as to what to do. Clients are finding their way to me; I am meeting like-minded people

and I have more time to do the things I love.
Thank you, Source. I handed over to the greater
power and I am receiving all my desires.

Methods for Attracting Positivity into Our Lives

There are several ways to deliberately change the
direction of our thoughts. **The key is to start** and then
have **a regular practise** to help us gradually effect
change in our thought patterns and belief systems.

1. Creative Visualisation Exercises

These help us to re-programme our thoughts in
a positive, creative way. They allow us to focus on
positivity, which simultaneously raises the frequency
of our energetic vibrations. Examples of these are the
creative exercises in Chapter Three and the Appendix:

- The Breathing in Peace Meditation
- The Sun Visualisation
- The Source Connection Visualisation
- Positive Affirmations – such as 'Every day,
  in every way, I am becoming stronger and
  healthy'.
- A specific, constructed visualisation

If we have negative thought patterns it helps to do
our chosen exercise(s) regularly. We could start before
we get up in the morning (or as soon as we can) as this
helps to set up our thought patterns for the day. Also,
every time we go to the toilet! This acts as a regular

reminder at a time when we are likely to be alone, throughout the day.

These short exercises are extremely effective at raising our energetic frequency.

2. **Affirmations**

Another effective way of consciously shaping our thoughts and creating a change in our reality, is through affirmations. We have discussed these already in Chapter Three when we talked about their use in visualisation exercises, but they can be so helpful in raising our energetic vibrations that we want to go into them in more detail here. For them to be really effective, there are a number of guidelines:

- Be specific and aim to only change one thing at a time. It is not helpful to list a series of changes that are needed
- Keep the affirmation simple and express only one thought, e.g. 'I am a peaceful person'
- Use only positive wording (see Chapter Three for a discussion about the importance of this)
- Accept the change now and use the present (rather than the future) tense to allow the energy of the thought to be brought into reality straightaway. For example, to help us get a job we would really like, we might say: 'Thank you that I am working in my dream job'
- Keep the focus on yourself. It is not helpful to blame others. We need to accept responsibility

for the reality we have currently created. If we feel unappreciated and unloved, the responsibility for this lies with us. We might say, 'I love myself and am worthy of being loved' which will positively influence our vibrational output as this new reality gains momentum

- Feel the joy now! Joy is of a high vibration and it will attract like energy into our lives
- Do repeat the affirmation constantly throughout the day. We are creating a thought form, which needs positive energy to become real. We need to keep saying it until every part of us believes and feels it
- Give it time. Our negative way of thinking is probably long-standing. Having patience and persistence with the affirmation will reverse the process
- Fake it till you make it! Reinforce the affirmation by acting as if this new way of thinking is true. For example, act as if you are confident if a change in your self-esteem is needed. You may be pleasantly surprised at the response from others which will, in turn, boost your self-esteem even further
- Trust that the change will happen
- Give thanks for the changes as soon as you have stated your affirmation as this strengthens the positive thought that change has already occurred

By following these guidelines, affirmations can be simple, but very valuable tools in raising our vibrations and so creating a more positive reality.

3. **Meditation**

Through meditation we can let our minds quieten and still and allow our peaceful beingness to permeate into our lives.

There are many different types of meditation. For example, Transcendental, Raj Yoga, Breath focused, Mantra, Zen, Mindfulness, Mettā, etc. If you would like to try meditation, then the best thing is to try a few different types and see which suits you best.

The benefits of meditation have been well researched and include a sense of calm and inner peace, but also many physical benefits.

On the downside, meditation tends to take time to practise and many people find that this prevents them from fitting it into their busy lives. The short visualisation exercises listed earlier can be repeated more frequently and we have found that they can yield similar results to a meditation practise.

4. **Gratitude and Appreciation**

Gratitude works energetically by strengthening our human energy field and simultaneously raising our vibrational frequency. Others cannot help but be drawn to someone who radiates the energy of gratitude as it is of a high vibration, extending outwards to all.

Heartfelt and spontaneous gratitude - even for

the small things in life - for example, someone we admire or respect, a pet, a much-loved possession, a favourite plant or tree in the garden or a favourite comfy armchair, gently transforms all things positively, including our physical environment.

Appreciation - The subtle shift from gratitude to appreciation involves being more present – more thoughtfully aware and active - in reflecting on the reasons why we feel grateful about something or someone. For example, we can be grateful for having food on our table. However, we can go further and appreciate its beauty, fragrance, taste, nutrition, and preparation.

Appreciation is a spiritual outlook which allows us to fill our hearts with joy. We can look at the wonders of planet Earth, focus on the marvels of nature and the positives in our lives. Practising gratitude and appreciation are great ways to improve our point of attraction for positive manifestation.

One way of doing this, is through keeping a Gratitude Journal in which we can write down specific things that we are grateful for every day.

A study by Seligman and colleagues, in 2005, invited participants to do an exercise called 'Three Good Things' which involved keeping a journal devoted solely to the positives in their lives. The participants were asked to write down three good things that had happened to them each day, for 10 minutes daily for a week, and afterwards they reported feeling happier and less depressed than when they started. In fact, they maintained their happiness boost six months later, illustrating how impactful it can be to focus on the good things in life.

5. Abraham's Twenty 'Deliberate Creation' Exercises

These twenty exercises are tailored to peoples' current emotional level, to help improve their point of attraction and are outlined in the book, *Ask and It Is Given – Learning to Manifest Your Desires* (Hicks 2004).

6. Joe Dispenza's Creation Process

Dr Joe Dispenza is a medical doctor, scientist, and teacher. He writes that people can work towards a higher vibrational frequency and a more coherent energetic state through meditation and visualisations. In so doing, if they then enter the quantum field (which exists beyond space and time) as pure consciousness, they can, with a knowing intent, attract the desired potential experience. His book, *Becoming Supernatural: How Common People are Doing the Uncommon* describes his suggested process for achieving this in detail (Dispenza, 2017).

7. Being Unconditional Love

If we travel within ourselves to understand our true nature (see Chapter One), and so allow our conscious thinking to reflect this understanding of ourselves as being part of Source, who is Unconditional Love, then we will emanate that high vibrational energy and attract high vibration into our lives.

Summary and Implications

We are not victims of fate. We are responsible for the quality of our lives and have the power to transform our reality through our thoughts.

Our emotions indicate our vibrational frequency and so an awareness of our emotions is a guide to the level of vibration we are emitting and therefore, what we are attracting into our lives.

High vibrational (positive) thoughts and actions not only create a better reality for ourselves, but because we are energetic beings and connected to all, we also positively impact society and our world – a powerful thought!

CHAPTER SIX

We Choose this Life!

Perhaps we have more influence on the lives we lead than we realise? Certain widely accepted theories point to us being less a victim in our lives and more of an architect: The Principles of Reincarnation, Karma[6] and the *Law of Attraction*.

Reincarnation

The word reincarnation is of Latin origin: *re*, meaning again and *incarnare*, meaning to make flesh. In other words, the rebirth of a soul in a new human body. Reincarnation is a core belief of many ancient and modern religions, tribal communities and mythology. Some believe that a person's karmic sum will decide the form they take in the next life.

Perhaps the most common and widely known example of a belief in reincarnation is the ancient Egyptians, whose excavated tombs reveal that the deceased were buried with food, clothing and other items deemed necessary in their next life.

In the West, reincarnation is mainly associated with 'New Age spirituality'. Due to the influence of Eastern gurus, the New Age movement arose and, as a result, there is a wider acceptance of reincarnation in our society today. Many of us may have recognised 'old souls' in babies or children. We'll say things like 'she's wise beyond her years' or 'I'm sure he's been here before.' These children will often spontaneously refer to other lives but are sometimes silenced by parents who don't understand the phenomenon.

An adult describes:

> I was recently told by a medium that I used to be a healer in ancient Egypt. That is probably why I have been drawn to study Egyptian history.

Those who accept the concept of reincarnation usually believe that the soul is immortal and eternal, that it exists to evolve and reach perfection by continually reincarnating until finally being free of karmic influences. This eventually allows a soul's ascension to a higher spiritual level. There are various different versions of how many lifetimes are needed to achieve this and what form they might take, depending on which belief system is embraced. The specifics vary enormously, but they share common themes of reincarnation and karma being connected.

When doing spiritual healing some healers are

occasionally shown aspects of a client's previous life which are impinging on the present one. For example, they might see an old-fashioned sword or dagger embedded in the part of the body where the client is currently feeling pain. The pain disappears once the energetic representation of the offending weapon is removed by Source.

> I remember one lady who came to me for healing and who was complaining of headaches in the top, left side of her head. During the session, in my mind's eye, I saw a sword sticking out of that area. I asked that it be safely removed if appropriate. After I had finished the energy rebalancing, the lady spontaneously told me that she had felt something being removed from that area. Afterwards, her headaches stopped.

Karma (The Principle of Cause and Effect)

The concept of karma originated in ancient India. The term itself is a Sanskrit word which means action, work or deed. It also refers to *the Principle of Cause and Effect*, where intent and actions of an individual or individuals (cause), influence the future of that individual or individuals (effect). Karma is usually, but not always, linked to reincarnation. Several types of karma are documented e.g. National Karma, Racial Karma, Planetary Karma, Universal Karma. We are going to focus on Individual Karma which is created by one person and affects that one person, though he or she can also be influenced by their environment, family, national or worldly occurrences.

Karma is based on the notion that every action has a consequence. Loosely defined, this means that good intentions and deeds create positive karma and future happiness, while bad intentions and deeds create negative karma and future suffering. Karma is not only connected to the relationship between actions and consequences, but also the moral reasons or intentions behind actions. So, if someone does a good deed for the wrong reasons - for example, a good deed done purely to impress someone else - the action would be self-serving and may not have the desired results.

The theory of karma plays an important part in many religions including Hinduism, Buddhism, Jainism and Sikhism, each one having its own interpretation and understanding of the concept.

There are a number of commonly used Western religious and non-religious phrases which draw parallels with karma, including 'You reap what you sow' and 'What goes around comes around', so most people are already familiar with the *Law of Cause and Effect* to some degree.

When associated with reincarnation, both positive and negative karma can be accrued, ready to be paid off in the form of a 'karmic debt' in another life.

For some people life can seem overly negative and unfair, but karmic influences could be the reason for this. For example, an individual who faces a constant stream of negative experiences in their current life, even though all their thoughts and actions are seemingly kind and well intentioned, could be repaying a negative karmic debt from another life. The reverse applies to someone who seems to have a continuously positive existence in their current life, despite being unkind or unpleasant in many ways; they could be benefitting from previously accrued positive karma. The *Law of Cause and Effect* is always in action, so any thoughts or actions intended to harm or negatively affect another must eventually be experienced by the perpetrator in some form – simply put: 'What goes around comes around'. Even if it is not necessarily in this lifetime!

The *intention* behind any action is one of the main elements of karmic creation

We are largely unaware of how long ago we acquired the karma that is manifesting in our current life. It is impossible to predict how or when the karma we create today will manifest as consequences. If you feel that your intentions, thoughts or actions are likely to have created negative karma, you may be comforted to know that remedial action can be taken! Your present positive actions may offset previous negative ones and create balance. This can be anything that requires you to act or give selflessly for the benefit of others, done with humility, a willing heart and without an ulterior motive.

Each time we react to even the smallest event, we need to be aware of the **intention** behind the action, as this is regarded as one of the main elements of karma creation. Our response to every situation is up to us; an awareness that karma is always being played out can inspire us to make any necessary changes to our thought patterns and beliefs. Since we are thinking, feeling, human beings who constantly interact with others, our perceptions and sense of wellbeing can fluctuate wildly; constantly leading to actions and reactions. And so, the cycle continues as we constantly create both positive and negative karma in every waking moment.

Our response to every situation is up to us

Karma as a Learning Tool, Not a Punishment

There is also another, more spiritual, explanation of karma. Although negative karma usually results in suffering of some kind, it doesn't need to be viewed as punishment or reward in the usual sense. If we are spiritually developed and sufficiently aware, karma can be seen simply as an opportunity to make amends, or even as spiritual guidance; it can help us to learn from our mistakes.

Karma is a spiritual re-balancing which can help us learn from our mistakes

In this context karma may also be used as an opportunity to experience something from a different perspective; to create balance and understanding on our human journey. Karmic debts can be viewed as debts owed to the self, their resolution helping our soul to progress spiritually. Thinking of karma as a form of energy re-balancing in which we take positive action to redress our (karmic) imbalance, puts the onus on the individual to achieve the re-balancing. It is not blind fate which thrusts circumstances on us as a kind of punishment. Karma can more positively be described as a spiritual re-balancing of our energetic beingness, rather than a price to be paid for wrongdoing.

Is Karma the same as The Law of Attraction?

No, they are actually very different. Depending on the belief system of the individual involved:

Karma is either a set of events and challenges

designed to assist the growth of the soul, pre-agreed before rebirth, or the result of cause and effect in the current life.

The Law of Attraction is:

a) *About mental focus* – The basic premise of *the Law of Attraction* (and *the Law of Vibration*) is that like energy attracts like energy. Our dominant energetic frequency is determined by our dominant mental attitude, which itself is determined by our habitual thoughts and beliefs.

b) *About choosing our vibrational frequency* - What we attract to ourselves is what we are in vibrational harmony with. So, if we want love and peace in our lives, we must become love and peace.

The two can function simultaneously by using the *Law of Attraction* to bring us a maximum sense of contentment, whatever our situation in life. For example, if we feel we are stuck in negative circumstances because of karmic influences, whilst we are working through them we can use the *Law of Attraction* to create a positive outlook (by focusing mainly on the things that make us feel good).

Soul Journeys and Choices

The work of psychotherapists and hypnotherapists such as Dolores Cannon, Dr Michael Newton and Dr Brian Weiss provide very convincing, detailed case studies of clients' past life regressions, which suggest that karma and reincarnation are a reality. They describe accounts of people who, under hypnosis for past life regression, have been taken back to the time between lives and these people describe remarkably similar experiences after the death of a physical body, when the soul is said to return 'home'. These reports, for example, state that on arrival, souls returning from extremely difficult lives or traumatic deaths may go to a place of rest, recuperation and healing. In addition, there are many processes and procedures to be dealt with, including reunions with soul groups, guides and a review of the actions and outcomes of their most recent life.

We make choices at soul level about the kind of life we wish to experience - for our learning or to teach

It is apparently common to reincarnate within the same soul group. So, we might be the mother to our son in this life and the soul of this son may be our aunt in another life! This is rather reassuring as it means we do not really ever lose close family or friends when they die. They are usually in the same soul group and are likely to be there to greet us when we transition.

> As healers, we have been privileged to observe this many a time when we do 'soul midwifery' for souls who have lost their way back home after their physical body dies and they are left wandering the Earth plane. Maybe they had the view that they did not want to leave their loved ones on Earth or felt that they had unfinished business when they died. Regularly, when we direct the lost soul back to the soul world, we see family and friends waiting to lovingly greet them upon their return. It is always a very moving sight.

Making Life Choices at Soul Level

It is said that prior to a soul's rebirth into the physical dimension, the soul makes choices about their next life: what gender they are to be; who will be their parents, siblings and partners; lessons to be learnt in the next life; appropriate circumstances to be born into to best learn and experience those lessons. With the help of spiritual 'Elders', there is carefully planned selection from several available options. Karmic agreements or 'contracts' are formed and close relationships in life usually involve specific pairings to work out particular karmic issues between souls.

So, for example, an individual who is physically

or mentally abused in a lifetime may well have had a soul contract with the perpetrator prior to that birth; perhaps a soul who, in another lifetime, the individual concerned had harmed and who, for the learning/ experience of both souls, was willing to act as the perpetrator this time round? Food for thought! This way of thinking certainly helps if we are trying to forgive somebody for something unpleasant done to us.

There are various levels of soul evolution, from beginner or novice right through to very advanced. Very advanced souls with no remaining karmic residue can choose to reincarnate solely to assist others. So-called Indigo, Crystal and Rainbow children are said to be advanced souls who are on a mission to help humanity create a peaceful, loving world.

Summary and Implications

Karma and reincarnation are complex, difficult topics for the human mind to understand fully. They are probably impossible to scientifically prove or disprove. Some people are unable to grasp the concept and remain mystified by it; others are total skeptics. If we are not bound by religious beliefs, it remains solely an individual choice of whether to accept and work with the concept or reject it.

Indeed, karma and reincarnation may not be the only reasons for the good fortune or challenges we experience in our lives, but a belief in them can answer questions such as:

> *What am I doing here?*
> *What is the purpose of all this?*
> *Why me?*
> *What did I do to deserve this?*

Understanding our experiences in terms of karma and reincarnation can help us to be content with our lot; it can also explain the extremes we observe in the world. For example, some people are robust and have constant good health, but others face a life of disability or pain; some are fabulously wealthy while others are homeless, starving and so on.

Important points to remember about karmic influences:

- Karma is not always negative
- As physical beings, we have no way of knowing where we stand on the karmic 'ladder', so working towards a way of being which creates positive karma is always worthwhile.
- By simply recognising that everything in the Universe - including thoughts, intentions, words and actions - is energy, we can choose to empower ourselves with positive, loving thoughts and benefit from the principles of karma. Love and forgiveness are thought to be vital components of karmic resolution. When

we allow love and forgiveness to be second nature, the result can be mental and emotional freedom and this, in turn, may contribute to easier resolution of specific karmic issues with other souls.

It is also very helpful to know that we make choices at soul level, for our learning or to teach, about the kind of life we are going to lead. This understanding helps to make sense of occurrences which on the surface seem unfair or when we feel that we are a victim of fate. We chose to have these experiences, even though when we are in the physical body it would seem an unlikely thing to do! When deciding as a soul and seeing our progress over many lives it makes sense.

CHAPTER SEVEN

More About Looking After Ourselves

– Because it is so important!

It is incredibly important that we take time and effort to look after ourselves.

So many people think that to be a kind, spiritual person they need to 'give their all' to others. If we understand that we are energetic beings, then giving our all means that our own vibration dips and, unless we spend time to recover this, we are going to have low energy ourselves and not be in a position to help anyone. Rather, it is us who will be in need of assistance. So, to be in the best position to help others we need to first look after our own energies.

Increasing our Resilience

Challenges to our stability in life are inevitable, but it is our capacity to cope with stress and regain our balance quickly, that enables us to lead constructive and fulfilling lives.

In the section of our Healer Foundation Course that covers how stress affects the human body, we do an exercise in which we hand students a number of small, toy balls (which are meant to represent the stresses in their lives) and ask them, one by one to put them into a small container which the tutor is holding. Inevitably, the container soon becomes full and the balls start to spill over and fall onto the floor. At this stage, the tutor pours the balls from the small container into a larger one which holds them all with room to spare, then asks the students what they think this represents.

The idea is that the students come up with the answer that the containers represent our capacity (or lack of it) to cope with the stresses in our lives. When we have little capacity to cope, our problems start to overwhelm us and spill out into our decision making and ability to thrive. When we do have capacity, we can much more easily cope with the challenges we are likely to encounter in life.

We can boost our power to face life's adversities by:

a) **increasing our self-nurturing** and so **increasing our capacity to cope** (developing a larger bucket)

b) **changing the way we think about problems** (making the balls (stresses) smaller). External problems have less impact if we have a more positive and realistic view of them. This reframing is a powerful cognitive tool and is often described as whether we see a glass as half full or half empty.

We can help ourselves by increasing our capacity to cope through self-nurturing and reframing the way we think about problems in life

Practical Ways to Increase our Capacity to Cope with Stress (Develop a larger bucket)

1. *Exercise*

Just about any form of physical activity can help relieve stress and burn away anger, tension, and frustration. Exercise releases endorphins that boost mood and can also serve as a valuable distraction to daily worries.

Maximum benefit comes from exercising for 30 minutes or more daily. Short, 10-minute bursts of activity that elevate our heart rate and make us break out into a sweat can help to relieve stress and give us more energy and optimism.

If we pick an activity we enjoy, we are more likely to continue with it.

By exercising mindfully, focusing on our body and the physical (and sometimes emotional) sensations we experience as we're moving, we can help to break out of the cycle of negative thoughts that often accompany overwhelming stress.

Furthermore, as exercise helps to raise our energetic vibration, we are likely to find it easier to put other stress management techniques to use.

2. *Sharing Problems*

Social engagement is the quickest, most efficient way to rein in stress and avoid overreacting to internal or external events that we perceive as threatening. There is nothing more calming to the nervous system than communicating with another human being who makes us feel safe and understood. It can halt defensive stress responses like 'fight-or-flight' and can also release 'feel-good' chemicals that reduce stress, even if we're unable to alter the stressful situation itself.

It is good to share our problems and how we are feeling and coping with a relative, friend, counsellor, doctor, or spiritual leader. The lonelier and more isolated we are, the greater our vulnerability to stress. On the flip side, by building and maintaining a network of close friends we can improve our resilience to life's stressors.

The people we talk to don't have to be able to fix

our problems; they just need to be good listeners. Opening up is not a sign of weakness and it won't make us a burden to others. In fact, most friends will be flattered that we trust them enough to confide in them, and it is likely to strengthen the friendship.

3. *Avoid Unnecessary Stress*
The following strategies are helpful:

- *Learning how to say 'no'.* Knowing our limits and sticking to them. Whether in our personal or professional life, taking on more than we can handle is a recipe for stress.
- *Avoiding people who stress us out.* If someone consistently causes stress in our lives, we need to limit the amount of time we spend with them or end the relationship.
- *Taking control of our environment.* For example, if the evening news makes us anxious, we can turn off the TV. If traffic makes us tense, whenever possible we can take a longer but less-travelled route.

4. *Calm our mind through meditation or visualisation exercises*
There is much research describing the benefits of meditation to reduce stress. However, we find that visualisation exercises are generally easier for people to do and get them to an emotional place of calm much quicker than meditation. (See Chapter Three

and the Appendix for useful and effective visualisation exercises, to positively manage our personal energy field).

5. *Make time for fun and relaxation*

We can reduce stress in our lives by nurturing ourselves. If we regularly make time for fun and relaxation, we'll be in a better place to handle life's stressors. Nurturing ourselves is a necessity, not a luxury.

- *Setting aside relaxation time* - including rest and relaxation in our daily schedule is important, as is not allowing other obligations to encroach on this. Giving ourselves time to relax and take a break from all responsibilities and recharge our batteries, is vital for our wellbeing
- *Doing something we enjoy every day* - making time for leisure activities that bring us joy helps to raise our energetic vibration
- *Keeping our sense of humour* - this includes the ability to laugh at ourselves! Laughter, apart from being fun, strengthens our immune system, lowers our stress hormones, and boosts our mood. So, find something that makes you laugh and do it often!
- *Doing something creative* - from how we wear our clothes or do our hair, rearranging the contents of a shelf or cupboard in the house, to writing a book or poem, painting or drawing

Nurturing ourselves is a necessity, not a luxury

6. *Adopt a healthy lifestyle*

In addition to regular exercise, there are other healthy lifestyle choices that can increase our resistance to stress:

- *Eating a healthy diet* - well-nourished bodies are better prepared to cope with stress, so it is good to be mindful of what we eat. Starting our day with a healthy breakfast and keeping our energy up and our mind clear with balanced, nutritious meals throughout the day helps to support us physically
- *Reducing caffeine and sugar* - the temporary 'highs' caffeine and sugar provide often end with a crash in mood and energy. By reducing the amount of coffee, soft drinks, chocolate, and sugary snacks in our diet, we'll feel more relaxed and sleep better
- *Avoiding alcohol, cigarettes and drugs* - self-medicating with alcohol or drugs may provide an easy escape from stress, but the relief is only temporary. Rather than avoiding or

masking the issue, it is more helpful to deal with problems head on and with a clear mind

- *Getting enough sleep* - adequate sleep fuels our mind, as well as our body. Feeling tired increases our stress because it may cause us to think irrationally (Walker 2018)

Changing the Way We Think about Problems (Make the balls of stress smaller)

Major life events are easy to identify as sources of stress, but what about peoples' own thoughts, feelings, and behaviours that contribute to stress levels?

1. *Alter Our Attitude to the Stressful Situation*

To identify our true sources of stress, we need to look closely at our habits, attitude, and excuses:

- Do you explain away stress as temporary ('I just have so many things going on right now'), though you can't remember the last time you took a break?
- Do you define stress as an integral part of your work or home life ('Things are always crazy around here') or as a part of your personality ('I'm just a nervy person that's all')?
- Do you blame your stress on other people or outside events, or view it as entirely normal?

We need to accept responsibility for the role we

play in creating or maintaining our stresses. Our mind is creating our world as stated in the maxim, 'as within, so without'.

The way we think can have a profound effect on our stress levels. It is helpful to regain our sense of control by changing our expectations and attitude to stressful situations:

- *Reframe problems.* Try to view stressful situations from a more positive perspective. Rather than fuming about a traffic jam, look at it as an opportunity to pause and be calm; we can listen to a favourite radio programme or enjoy some alone time. (Though don't try to meditate whilst driving. No point in being Zen but causing a traffic accident!)
- *Look at the big picture.* Take perspective of the stressful situation. Ask how important it will be in the long run. Will it matter in a month? A year? Is it really worth getting upset over? If the answer is no, it is a good idea to focus our time and energy elsewhere
- *Adjust our standards.* Perfectionism is a major source of avoidable stress. We need to set reasonable standards for ourselves and others and learn to be okay with 'good enough' where appropriate. It makes life so much easier

2. *Adapt to the Stress*

If we can't avoid a stressful situation, we can try

to alter the way we deal with it. Often, this involves changing the way we communicate and do things in our daily life:

- *Expressing our feelings instead of bottling them up* - if something or someone is bothering us, we can be more assertive and communicate our concerns in an open and respectful way. If we don't voice our feelings, resentment will build, and the stress will just increase
- *Be willing to compromise* - when we ask someone to change their behaviour, we need to be willing to do the same. If we are both willing to bend at least a little, we'll have a better chance of finding a happy middle ground
- *Manage our time better* - poor time management can cause a lot of stress. If we plan ahead and make sure we don't overextend ourselves, we'll find it easier to stay calm and focused. We may feel under pressure due to work deadlines, but at times it may be our procrastination, rather than the actual job demands, that is causing the stress

3. *Accept the things we can't change*

Many sources of stress are unavoidable. We can't prevent or change stressors, such as the death of a loved one, a serious illness, a pandemic or a national recession. In such cases, the best way to cope with stress is to accept things as they are. Acceptance may be difficult, but in the long run, it's easier than kicking against a situation we can't change:

- *Don't try to control the uncontrollable* - many things in life are beyond our control. Rather than stressing over them, focus on the things we can control such as the way we choose to react to problems
- *Look for the upside* - when facing major challenges, try to look at them as opportunities for personal growth. If our own poor choices contributed to a stressful situation, reflect on them and learn from mistakes
- *Break the cycle of negative thoughts* – by realising that it is not what has happened to us or what was done to us which is affecting us now, it is the thoughts we are currently having about the past situation. When our thoughts are winding us up it helps to accept that the only person who is being hurt by our negative thought pattern is us – we are continuing and escalating the hurt through our thoughts. When we decide to stop and break the cycle of blame and anger and concentrate on thoughts which are more positive, (such as doing a positive affirmation or visualisation) we start to raise our energetic vibration and life becomes easier. We have this choice
- *Learn to forgive* - accept the fact that we live in an imperfect world and that people (including

ourselves) make mistakes. If we can let go of anger and resentments, we can free ourselves from negative energy by forgiving and moving on with our lives (The important issue of forgiveness is discussed further in Chapter Eight)

- *Live in the Present* – our vibrational frequency dips if our thoughts are focused on regretting things about a past event that we cannot change or dreading a future which might never happen. Living fully in the now allows us to feel calm and enjoy life (Tolle 1999)

Summary and Implications

It is extremely important for our health and our ability to cope with the stresses in life that we take time for ourselves. Taking the two-pronged approach to a) increase our capacity to cope with stress by self-care (increase the size of the container) and b) change the ways we think about our problems (decrease the size of the balls of stress), helps us to maintain a high energetic vibration.

If we want to create a better reality for ourselves, a highly vibrating energy field is the essential starting point. Looking after ourselves is not selfish, it is a necessity for an enjoyable life and positively impacts on those close to us, wider society and our world.

CHAPTER EIGHT

Forgiveness = Spiritual Growth

Although we may be aware that forgiveness is a good thing spiritually, many people find it impossible to get past the anger and deep hurt they feel regarding negative events in their lives which, in their opinion, are created by others. This can prevent them from even contemplating forgiveness, let alone moving towards it. Once we do allow ourselves to reach the point of considering forgiveness, we are often unsure how to go about it or fear that to forgive means that we are 'going soft', or that it will leave us open to attack from others.

Forgiveness cannot be achieved by just willing it to be done, there needs to be a shift in perspective within us and a turning away from the issues which have bound us to the person or situation concerned; to recognise the pain we suffered without letting that pain define us.

According to Buddhist teachings, every situation and object only acquires meaning when we contemplate it. It's helpful to stand back from the issue and observe the bigger picture, involving how our perception of this situation or person has clouded our thoughts and emotions; how it chains us to past attitudes and thought patterns. When we deeply desire our mind and heart to release the pattern of resentment and blame and accept the way things are, just as they are, we can start to take responsibility for our lives and move forwards.

When we take responsibility for our lives, we can move forwards

Putting Forgiveness into Perspective

If we see ourselves as victims, we will remain always as victims as the Universe will support us in that belief. When we view a painful experience from the place of victimisation, we are not seeing through the eyes of the higher self; the place of who we are in truth.

To forgive is to know ourselves and make spiritual progress, achieving mastery of our emotions. It dissolves the burden of painful memories and transforms them into spiritual understanding. Forgiveness = Spiritual Growth.

The Benefits of Forgiveness

It is now widely accepted that the weight of unresolved issues such as regret, hatred, jealousy, bitterness, trauma, grief, anger, pain and fear all add to the density of the burden we carry in our energy field and lower the frequency of our energetic vibrations. The more unfinished business, the denser our energy fields, the lower our vibrational frequency and the longer we must wait for change to occur in our lives.

Choosing to shed this energetic weight means we can add lightness to our energy fields and raise our energetic frequency to make way for new, lighter, happier experiences and spiritual progression.

Simply put, by forgiving the so-called offender and having the wisdom and humility to recognise that they have given us an opportunity to grow spiritually, we benefit. Forgiveness is a gateway to healing, love, light, health and happiness.

Refusal to forgive can affect our health as it is linked to various energetic imbalances and dis-ease (Hay 2005). This makes forgiveness one of the most important activities for the healing of the self. It allows us to move from fear and emotional clouding to compassion, mental equilibrium, wisdom and love. It is the doorway to self-knowledge and self-awareness, and it is valuable for both the forgiver and the forgiven.

Louise Hay writes (2005, p70):

> '*Love is always the answer to healing of any sort.* And the pathway to love is forgiveness. Forgiveness dissolves resentment.'

The philosopher, David Whyte (2015), writes that forgiveness is an act of compassion and is one in which we become a bigger person than the aspect of our self who was first wounded. We need, with maturity, to bring about an identity which can embrace our hurt and the memories associated with it, but also extend our understanding to the one who wounded us.

The Energy of Forgiveness

As we are aware, energy transfers (Chapter Three), so people who perpetuate negative emotions such as resentment, bitterness, hatred and envy may also cause relationship problems when this undercurrent of negativity is sensed by those they share their lives with, for example their partner or children. It can also negatively affect the energy field of the person for whom they harbour those thoughts and emotions. Knowingly seeking to punish the one we view as a perpetrator in this way means that the negative energy may come back to us in the karmic process of cause and effect. (Chapter Six).

Forgiveness may not immediately change our feelings towards people, but it will allow us to start the process of severing our past connections and re-directing our energy into getting on with our current lives. Enabled to feel happier, more contented and at peace with our lives, through forgiveness, we can learn and grow in spiritual stature.

Forgiving Others

It is important that forgiving others is not done as an exercise of power in which we show that we can rise above the incident publicly, but privately never forget it. When we behave self-righteously, we harm ourselves and separate ourselves energetically from our fellow human beings.

In the process of forgiving, the willingness of the mind and the intent to forgive is important. Consider that the other person may have lashed out because they were feeling wounded, confused or vulnerable themselves at the time. They may even believe that they are the victim.

We can choose love or fear

It can be helpful to understand that at the base of ALL negative emotions (such as anger, depression, jealousy, guilt, hatred) is always fear (A Course in Miracles, 2007). In reality, our lives are dominated by only two emotions – love and fear. It is fear of someone or some event that can result in judgement of another.

We can choose love or fear. The consequence of choosing fear is suffering, whereas choosing an emotion founded on love lightens us and results in contentment and peace.

We do not need to feel actual love itself or respect for the person, or to condone their actions. We are simply viewing the situation as a soul, with an expanded perspective and allowing ourselves to feel better and experience lightness of being. If we are able to view the offending words or circumstances as a tool for our spiritual growth, we may become aware of the true purpose of being involved in the situation and take from it what we need to move forwards. Our job is not to judge others, but to act with the unconditional love of our higher self.

Louise Hay (2005) writes that the person you find hardest to forgive is the one you need to forgive the most. She explains that forgiveness means letting go, not condoning behaviour. All we need is to be willing to do it.

It's not a sign of weakness to admit that you are not mentally or emotionally in the right place to practise forgiveness. It is essential, rather than half-heartedly attempting it because you feel it's the right thing to do, then feeling even worse about the person or situation concerned afterwards.

If you are not ready to forgive someone for something very damaging they did to you, Martin

(2014) writes that it is helpful to accept that this is how you feel at the moment and reconcile yourself with that. Give yourself the time you need to recover and restore your faith in others. With continued practise of forgiving lesser hurts, it may be possible for you to proceed to the more challenging ones in time. You may need to do what he calls 'Tough Forgiveness' which involves giving yourself permission not to have any future relationship with the other person unless certain conditions are met by them.

Tools for Starting the Forgiveness Process

Even if you've reached the point of willingness to forgive yourself or someone else, it's clearly not just a matter of having the thought and then it's done. When you feel that your heart and mind are sufficiently ready to attempt forgiveness, the method you use needs to be meaningful to *your* particular circumstances and appropriate for adaptation into *your* life. Below are just a few of the methods available out there.

Many people benefit from identifying their pain and/or anger and then processing it safely in the present moment. This could be via one of a number of recognised methods for releasing emotional hurt such as:

1. **Writing your feelings down on paper,** then tearing it into tiny pieces and discarding it,

simultaneously allowing yourself to release any
associated pain

2. **Crying or screaming into a pillow** when no-
one is around

3. **Engaging in physical activity** to assist the
movement and release of stuck energy

Forgiveness is a choice

4. **A Creative Visualisation - Letting Go in
Forgiveness**

*This visualisation is a good one to start the
forgiveness process. It enables us to use our powers of
creative imagination to set the scene and visualise the
process of forgiveness, whilst not having to speak to
the person involved. This exercise can benefit both the
person forgiving and the receiver. The aim is to allow a
flow of unconditional love and forgiveness, while letting
go of any residual thoughts and emotions. There is no
need to revisit the painful memory. It is enough to know
that you wish to let it go.*

- Take a few deep abdominal breaths and relax
- Feel your feet on the ground, know that the
  Earth is supporting you and breathe normally
  and easily. Allow yourself to become still,
  creating a sense of inner calmness
- Visualise yourself in a large, airy indoor space
  of quiet contemplation

- The space is separated into two parts by a special screen, which allows you to see through but provides total privacy from the other side. You are out of sight of anyone else
- You are sitting on a comfortable chair behind the screen
- If any negative thoughts or emotions come into your awareness, simply refuse to engage with them and allow them to dissipate
- The person concerned enters the far end of the space. From the seclusion of your location, you can see them, but they cannot see you nor can they approach you. You are completely safe
- They go to a nearby table, which has been laid out by you in advance with symbols of peace and unconditional love that would be meaningful to you and the other person, for example, candles, roses, or a rose quartz crystal heart
- Also on the table is a letter from you, explaining how you realise that the anger and resentment you have been feeling towards them has caused pain and suffering; that you are ready to forgive them, set yourself free and move on
- You recognise that they too are a soul on a physical journey, so the letter also invites them to choose one of the gifts from the table, from your higher self, as a token of unconditional love

- Then let the image fade away as the person leaves the building, not to return unless you invite them to do so on another occasion
- They now have the opportunity to make their own choices about how to deal with any residual pain or anger they themselves might be experiencing
- Feeling relieved, smiling and happy, you allow yourself to feel full of the Love of Source... (Pause)
- Now, bring your attention back to the soles of your feet and feel that connection with the Earth. Make sure that you are grounded and that your energies are now at an appropriate level for normal daily life. Open your eyes and give thanks for your transformed state of peace

If, after this visualisation, YOU ARE NOT FEELING FULLY GROUNDED or FEELING SPACED OUT do the following grounding exercise:

Sense the ground beneath your feet and feel the Earth supporting you.

If you feel that you need further grounding, put a hand on the top of your head and then imagine golden roots growing from the soles of your feet into the centre of the Earth. These roots are grounding your energies. When you feel ready, you can remove your hand from your head and open your eyes.

Or if you are not able to visualise or sense energy, you

can state your intention to be connected to the Earth and thank and know that this is the case.

5. **Four Steps to Forgiveness**

William Martin (2014) says that forgiveness is a choice. He describes an accessible tool to help us forgive called the *Four Steps to Forgiveness*:

Step 1 – State who you need to forgive and for what

Step 2 – Acknowledge, honestly, how you really feel about the situation at the moment. Then express your willingness to let go of these feelings (or at least be willing to consider the possibility of doing this)

Step 3 –Think about the benefits you will receive from forgiving. This is likely to be the opposite of what you are currently feeling, e.g. lightness instead of heaviness, peace instead of anger, etc.

Step 4 – Commit yourself to forgiving. Simply state who you intend to forgive and acknowledge the benefits which will come from this. For example: *I commit myself to forgiving XXX and I accept the peace and freedom which forgiveness brings*

6. **Ho 'oponopono**

Many people find that the ancient Hawaiian practise of forgiveness, Ho' oponopono, enhances the forgiveness process. There are varied interpretations of its literal meaning, but they are each based on the understanding that together we form the 'whole' while remaining individual (as discussed in Chapter One). If we choose to accept that: we create our own reality; that we have contributed to the problem in some way because we are interconnected; we take responsibility for our part in it and, we send out unconditional love from our higher self, it's possible not only to find personal inner peace but also to positively affect the 'whole' (which includes the person or situation that we are intending to forgive).

Miraculous results can be achieved by repeating the following four simple phrases:

I'm sorry. Please forgive me. Thank you. I love you.

A loose interpretation of each phrase is:

I'm sorry: I accept responsibility for causing the problem at some level (perhaps even in another lifetime)

Please forgive me: for my part in this

Thank you: for bringing this to my attention so that progress can be made

I love you: my higher self sends unconditional love to all concerned

The key to its success is practising it as frequently as needed, at any time of the day or night and actually *feeling* the words as you think or say them. It only takes a few repetitions to experience a sense of relief and a positive change to your emotional state.

Ho 'oponopono works particularly well with forgiveness but can be used in any challenging situation.

An example of how forgiveness can work in a miraculous way:

> As a healer, it was rather embarrassing that I had numerous small warts on the fingers of both my hands which I had had for about a year. Nothing I seemed to do would get rid of them.
>
> Eventually, I looked up in Louise Hay's book, *You can Heal your Life,* to see what thought pattern she believed that I was holding onto which might be causing them. She states that warts are physical manifestations of: *Little expressions of hate. Belief in Ugliness.*
>
> 'Well!', I thought, 'I don't hate anyone!'. Then I decided to have a deeper think about it and realised that perhaps I was annoyed at a couple of members of my family who had done things to upset me.
>
> Because I believe that we are all energetically connected and that at some level I had done something to cause my family members to act as they had, I decided to email them both and apologise and in my heart forgive them and send deep and unconditional love to them.
>
> The next morning, when I awoke, the warts had completely disappeared and have never returned!

Forgiving Ourselves

Forgiving ourselves can often be harder to do. It means, amongst other things, letting go of guilt surrounding what we feel were mistakes and, understanding that making mistakes is an important part of life. If we think of something that we feel guilty about, it can be helpful to consider what we have learnt from the experience. Perhaps we became aware of an aspect of ourselves that we didn't like, giving us the opportunity to change. If someone else made the same mistake, what would we say to them? '*Have you gained in wisdom from the experience? If so, it may be time to let go and move on.*'

Self-forgiveness is also useful early in the drama, rather than putting ourselves through the wringer of self-recrimination for a lengthy time until we finally acknowledge the learning arising from the mistake.

It is best if we don't give ourselves a hard time and carry guilt about something that we said or did. This can inhibit our energy flow and lower our vibration just as effectively as feeling anger and resentment towards someone else.

Consider the good which we can do from now on, rather than spending time thinking about the bad which we cannot undo. (Martin 2014). It is important to focus on progress in our spiritual development, not perfection. Expecting our negative attitudes and unhealthy thinking to change quickly isn't realistic. The only thing that matters is the direction we are moving in. Let us be patient with ourselves if we occasionally relapse into judgemental attitudes and bitterness towards another. It can be helpful to practise self-forgiveness often, as a reminder that through making mistakes, we can learn; practise makes it easier, until it eventually becomes second nature to us.

William Martin writes that self-forgiveness is a very un-selfish act as it frees us from inclinations towards self-centredness. It allows us to be a better version of ourselves and have positive relationships with others.

The self-love of allowing ourselves to celebrate our uniqueness, feeling love for everything that makes us who we are, can help with self-forgiveness. This includes loving all our self-perceived flaws and inadequacies (see Chapter Ten).

How to Forgive Ourselves

William Martin's *Four Steps to Forgiveness* can also be used to help self-forgiveness, by adding a section to Step 3 on how forgiving ourselves will benefit others too.

Psychologist, Fred Luskin PhD, explains that it is not what we feel guilty about from our past which causes us problems, but rather our current reactions to it and the resultant emotions that we feel now. Self-forgiveness allows us to move on with our lives.

The following exercise can help with self-forgiveness:

- Close your eyes, and do a couple of deep, abdominal breaths and then breathe normally
- Have the intention that it is time to forgive yourself
- Now visualise yourself in a beautiful, peaceful scene in nature. Relax and feel the peace of the surroundings
- Absorb these feelings of peace and calm into your inner being, your soul
- Know that this your true state of being, it is who you really are
- In this peaceful state, ask your inner being, your core of love and peace, what you can say or do to help with self-forgiveness
- You may receive knowledge about how to move forwards (which might, for example, be a subtle thought, an image in your mind's eye or simply a 'knowing')
- Know that you can act on this to forgive yourself, either in this moment or at some point in the future
- Now bring your attention back to the soles of your feet and feel that connection with the Earth. Make sure that that you are grounded and know that your energies are now at an appropriate level for normal daily life and when you are ready, open your eyes

If, after this visualisation, YOU ARE NOT FEELING FULLY GROUNDED or FEELING SPACED OUT do the following grounding exercise:

Sense the ground beneath your feet and feel the Earth supporting you.

If you feel that you need further grounding, put a hand on the top of your head and then imagine golden roots growing from the soles of your feet into the centre of the Earth. These roots are grounding your energies. When you feel ready, you can remove your hand from your head and open your eyes.

Or if you are not able to visualise or sense energy, you can state your intention to be connected to the Earth and thank and know that this is the case.

Summary and Implications

Forgiveness is a conscious choice.

Non-forgiveness involves the mind's refusal to accept a situation, past or present.

To forgive is to offer no resistance to life – to allow life energy to flow through us.

Blocking the flow of life will mean pain and suffering, a greatly restricted flow of life energy and often physical disease.

We need to accept what we cannot change, understand that there is or was a reason for the event or behaviour and let go of the emotions involved.

We can unblock the flow of our life's energy by releasing past events and negative reactions to them.

We can decide to accept what happened.

We can give thanks for the experience and the opportunity to expand our consciousness.

The moment we truly forgive from the heart, we reclaim our power from the mind.

CHAPTER NINE

Empaths, Sensitives and Intuition

In a nutshell, Empaths and Highly Sensitive People (sometimes referred to as HSPs) can have a difficult time coping with life, no matter what their circumstances. Some feel constantly bombarded by life, and suffer ill health accompanied by unfathomable lethargy. Most are misunderstood, sometimes feeling that they are 'going mad' without knowing that the real cause for their distress is their high sensitivity to the energies all around them in this energetic world.

> I have always struggled to cope with life because of my super-sensitivity to the energy of others and its associated challenges. I never understood why most of the time I felt drained and slightly unwell, until I found out that I was an Empath – this explained everything.

Although there are various types of Empaths and Sensitives, each with differing degrees of sensitivity, this chapter focuses on a general overview of their challenges and the possible benefits they can experience.

Highly Sensitive People 'feel' the energy of others to some degree on a regular basis which, in itself can be problematic at times.

Empaths experience the energies around them in extremely deep ways and they readily and unintentionally absorb things such as:

- the distress, pain or fear of other humans, animals, places and situations
- the souls of people who have died
- the negative energy of geographical locations

They can also be aware of catastrophic events occurring in places other than their immediate location, often at the other side of the world. They can be overly sensitive to sounds, smells, light etc., and usually dislike being with large groups of people. Many can communicate energetically with animals and nature.

Judith Orloff (2018) explains that you can be a Highly Sensitive Person and an Empath at the same time, but Empaths are higher on an energetic sensitivity spectrum. In general, they both share a love of nature, quiet environments, and often have a rich inner life.

There are many Empaths and Highly Sensitive People in our society, some being severely affected by what seems like a major ongoing life challenge. This may not only affect the Empath or Highly Sensitive Person themselves, it can also have a knock-on effect on the lives of those who are closely associated with them. Family members or other people who don't have this 'problem' may perceive the resultant, often debilitating consequences of such sensitivities as weakness and any coping strategies as awkward or anti-social traits.

Empaths and Sensitives can easily become overwhelmed with the constant input of energetic information received, whether from positive or negative vibrations.

> As someone who was born an Empath, super-sensitive to everyone and everything, I have always tried to shield myself from the bombardment of different energies around me (some positive but mostly negative) as best I could by going 'inwards'. Throughout my life this has led to me being perceived as 'difficult' or 'aloof'.
>
> I never really 'fitted in' at school, at work, with peers, or sometimes even with other family members (although they have tolerated my 'over sensitive nature' more than most).
>
> My attempts to remedy this only resulted in me coming across as more difficult or aloof than ever. I did what I could to fit in better but, because I wasn't being my true self, the extra effort of trying to be someone other than who I really am was very wearing. I ended up being reluctant to mix with others as I found most

situations at best abrasive, at worst downright unpleasant. Finding out that I could manage my sensitivities has made my life so much easier, but even now, I still prefer time alone in nature or in my own private space to anything else.

Self-Help Strategies

Firstly, it is good for Empaths and Sensitives to realise that they might not be psychiatrically ill and are simply very sensitive to energy. It helps for them to have the realisation that they are energetic beings living in an energetic world and that they feel this energy more than others; consequently they 'pick up' energies which do not rightfully belong to them which can give them strange sensations and/or make them become ill. When people become aware that this might be the case, it can help greatly for them to seek out a healer who is trained and experienced in clearing lower vibrational energies.

> Many years ago on a trip to an ancient castle in the UK, I visited the dungeon building, which at the time was accessed via a simple descent down some stone steps and not the guided, interactive experience it has subsequently become. I was ill prepared for what hit me energetically as I descended the steps and entered the actual dungeon area. I sensed an all-consuming energy of distress, fear, sadness and pain all rolled into one, almost knocking me over. I walked round the largest of the chambers, which displayed various ancient

instruments of torture and had a tiny barred, aperture very high up in one wall, allowing in only the tiniest shaft of daylight. I noticed a deep hole measuring approximately 2 feet x 2 feet square, set into the stone floor at the foot of a wall and covered by a heavy metal grid, almost like a fireplace. The notice above it said it was a prisoner isolation space. This area was particularly traumatic to me for some reason.

I reached a point where I found the collective, overwhelmingly dark, heavy energy of what had previously taken place there so devastatingly upsetting that I started to cry and decided to leave. Luckily, it was dark enough for the few other people in there not to notice the state I was in, so I just pretended I had a cold. It took me a good while to pull myself together afterwards and I needed some healing when I got home.

I have since learnt how to manage such experiences positively, including the use of powerful techniques such as the Source Connection Visualisation Exercise. (See Appendix).

Secondly, it is vital for Empaths and Highly Sensitive People to manage their energies - keeping the frequency of their energetic vibration high and protected and taking action if they feel it start to dip.

We regularly see clients who come to us for healing who know that 'something' is wrong, but for whom conventional medicine has not been able to explain their feelings of ill health. They are delighted when they are finally understood, and that we can suggest ways to help with their hyper-sensitivity symptoms. These strategies are discussed in Chapters Three and Seven and the Appendix.

It is extremely important that they take the time for themselves to remain highly vibrational, as this is the best protection against lower vibrational intrusions and, in some cases, the effects of their 'other lives' being sensed in their current life.

> I'd worked through a series of quite challenging circumstances which had left me feeling emotionally lower than usual.
>
> I woke up one morning with severe pain going from under my chin at the front, upwards towards the back of my head to where the base of my skull meets my neck. It encircled my whole throat and neck. This pain seemed very unusual, unlike anything I had ever experienced before; it was particularly bad under one side of my jaw.
>
> At the side where I had most discomfort I felt for a swollen gland, thinking that I was fighting an infection, but this seemed normal to the touch. I tried to work on the pain myself, using a couple of self-help techniques that had worked for me in the past, but it persisted and felt as if it was getting worse.
>
> In desperation I called a healer friend for her to do some distant healing for me. This healer was experienced in energetic clearing

work and during the session, she saw me as a short man wearing a hooded jacket, with a noose around my neck, in the process of being hanged. This image fitted the site of my pain exactly, the most intense part under my jawbone being caused by the knot of the noose.

She was also able to discern that this was a past/parallel life impinging on my current life, due to the recent dip in my vibration. As she cleared my energy field and worked on raising my energetic frequency, the pain melted away and I felt completely back to normal.

As an Empath, I totally accepted that this was a lesson in the importance of raising and maintaining my vibration at a high level, which protects me from lower vibrational energy intrusions.

Thirdly, thought intention is also an energy and is very powerful. Empaths and sensitive people, from a place of high vibration, have the power to use their thoughts to protect their energies. See Chapter Five for 'Methods for Attracting Positivity into Our Lives.' For example, they can regularly use an affirmation such as:

> *Thank you that my mind, body and spirit are filled with the highest vibration of Light and Love.*

In reality, much of what they are affected by is 'for their information' only and they are not required to respond, have an opinion or try to change anything if it doesn't involve them personally. If well managed, their sensitivities can be useful in true discernment of other people and situations.

Intuition

On the up-side, all types of Highly Sensitive People also tend to be very intuitive. Intuition can be described as instinctive feelings and knowledge which are not purely rational or logical, more commonly called hunches and synchronicities or a gut instinct. Most people have intuitive moments but tend to dismiss them as irrational thoughts, particularly when they are prompted to act in a way which isn't in keeping with what they have already planned. An Empath or Highly Sensitive Person (once they come to recognise their intuitive messages for what they are) can benefit from acting on these intuitive feelings and changing their plans accordingly. Gradually it becomes, by and large, how they live their lives.

We all have the ability to access the wisdom of an inner guiding 'voice' (sometimes also called the Higher Self, Source or 'The Holy Spirit') when we immerse ourselves in moments of stillness. If we would allow ourselves to become aware of them, signs and signals are available to us to guide us along our pathway, help in our creativity and offer wisdom. They may be subtle, such as hearing about the same book from different people which might prompt us to read it and receive guidance; or in stillness receive a 'knowing' about a course of action to take which we had not previously considered.

Being aware of the possibility of this inner guidance is the first step to being open to receiving it. Due to our connectedness with All That Is, we are all wiser than we might have thought!

Summary and Implications

Being an Empath or Highly Sensitive Person need not be debilitating. The techniques in this book, if regularly practised, can create and maintain a strong, highly vibrating energy field. This has a two-fold effect:

1. it helps them to avoid being on the same frequency as negative energy
2. it allows them to sense other energies without being affected by them

The self-management of their energy will allow the Empath or person with high sensitivity to enjoy their intuitive gifts, to be able to use them in a positive way and so enjoy life.

People who are not Sensitives can also benefit from tapping into the inner guidance that is available to everyone, if they accept that there is always unseen help at hand in the form of intuition. Recognising it for what it really is when it happens, instead of ignoring it, can help to make life easier.

CHAPTER TEN

Practically Applying Spiritual Principles to Life's Challenges

The whole point of this book is to explain how, if we apply the spiritual principles outlined, we can make life, with all its inevitable challenges, much easier for ourselves.

It is important for us to remember that we create our reality (Chapters Four and Five) and we need to take responsibility for this and not blame others for our unhappiness.

In this chapter we look at a variety of specific life challenges (in no particular order) and, whilst fully acknowledging how difficult these problems can be for people, look at them in a spiritual way. Such an outlook can make a huge difference in our ability to cope with and enjoy life. Nothing may change in appearance, yet everything changes. Our thoughts and beliefs about our challenges can be transformed from seeming overwhelming to being viewed with understanding, and so allowing us an easier outlook on life.

Relationship Problems

He is a complete idiot!
We can't seem to discuss anything without arguing.
The kids won't listen to a word I say.
She is just so bad-tempered all the time.

Do any of these seem familiar?

When dealing with a difficult relationship, it is helpful to remember that the close relationships we have in this life are chosen by us before we incarnate, perhaps so that we can work out particular karmic issues between us. Family members often incarnate together for precisely this reason and so it is no wonder that they can press our buttons!

If we consider ourselves to be working through negative karma within a physical relationship, we have a choice. We can either:

- react badly and add to it, making sure it comes up in another life together
- see it for what it is and help to resolve it by acting in a more appropriate way this time round, with love, which starts the ball rolling in the opposite direction and perhaps resolves the issue permanently

If you find someone shouting at you (whether someone close or not) you can do the quick Bubbles of Light Exercise (Appendix, Section D) so that your energetic vibration is not affected. Ask for loving energy (directly from Source, not from you) to fill the other person's bubble, knowing that this is transforming the energies within it.

This short exercise can be very powerful, transforming a situation of anger into one of reconciliation.

> My son and I were having one of our regular arguments. During the heated debate I thought, 'What am I doing?' I need to take responsibility here. This is my son. I need to move forwards. So, I did the Bubbles of Light exercise and asked that his bubble was filled with the loving Light of Source. As I watched, I was amazed how quickly the situation changed. He just stopped shouting. We looked at each other, both apologised and then hugged.
>
> I think if ever I was in doubt about whether these visualisation exercises worked, I stopped then and there!

Other explanations of why we might have difficult relationships are:

- We are energetic beings in an energetic world
- The *Law of Attraction*

The *Law of Attraction* (or Vibration) holds that all energy has a vibrational frequency and, as a result we attract energy that is a vibrational match to our own - rather like tuning a radio to a particular station.

This means that if our energetic frequency is low, we'll attract more negative people into our lives. Taking responsibility and action to raise our vibration (Chapters Three and Seven) and maintaining it at a high level will help us attract more pleasant people, because energetically, like attracts like. This is good to remember if we are looking for a partner or to make friends. In other words, we need to work on ourselves and not blame other people.

Similarly, our relationship with others is a reflection of the relationship we have with ourselves. Our thoughts about ourselves create our experience. If we are continually thinking negative and fearful thoughts, we attract that negativity into our lives. Chapter Five lists some ways of starting to attract positivity into our lives. All we need to do is to get started! (Hibbert, 2019).

Finally, when confronted by people who seem mean and unpleasant it helps to understand:

- that at the base of ALL negative emotions (such as anger, depression, jealousy, guilt, hatred) is always fear (Chapter Eight). We can choose to reply with love and dispel this negative emotion or perpetuate the fear
- the true magnificence of ALL people (Chapter One). This realisation is incredibly useful. The people concerned are likely to be acting from an outlook of the physical world with all its apparent problems and inconveniences. If,

however, we can look beyond the outer physical appearance of the person and their behaviour, and see them as the magnificent soul that they truly are (their energy of Unconditional Love) it helps to foster harmony and defuse situations. Our thoughts about them become highly vibrational and as a result, their manner changes positively. This is the true secret of harmonious relationships – regarding each other as the loving souls that we are, allows apparent discord on the physical level to dissolve and become unimportant

Love and forgiveness are thought to be vital components of karmic resolution. When we allow love and forgiveness to be second nature, this can contribute to easier resolution of specific karmic issues with other souls.

Put simply, love is always the answer to life's problems. If we apply love to any situation, (also remembering love for ourselves) we will then experience the unfolding of positivity in our lives!

The application of love is always the answer to any of life's problems

Feeling Worthless

Many people feel that they do not have value. This may be because of family or societal conditioning, guilt for perceived wrongs, or because they feel that they do not match up to media portrayal of the perfect person in terms of appearance or success in life.

Louise Hay, in her book 'You can Heal your Life' (2005) writes that WHATEVER problem people struggle with, the only thing she ever works with them on is SELF-LOVE. She says that when people love, accept and approve of themselves exactly as they are, then life works for them.

Starting to think of ourselves as an aspect of the Unconditional Love of Source (Chapter One) is a first step to loving ourselves. It helps to realise that it is not our outward appearance and situation in this projection of life which is important, but our spiritual progress. We have chosen this life to learn, teach or experience. What a brave soul to have chosen a 'less than ideal' life, appearance and situation! As aspects of Source, whatever our apparent outward life, our inner spiritual reality is rich and radiant with Unconditional Love.

We can start to reflect this reality into our lives when we embrace our energetic beingness and work to raise the frequency of our energetic vibrations. As the *Law of Vibration* brings like energy into our lives and, we continue to work on ourselves to raise our vibration and maintain this, the realisation of our true magnificence (self-love) becomes an automatic result.

Feeling Lonely

Feelings of loneliness or that others do not understand us are common. We find that it helps here to focus on who we really are:

- We are not just isolated humans existing on this planet for a relatively short period of time
- We are eternal, individualisations of magnificent, loving Source energy in human form

Consciously being aware of this allows us to realise our connectedness to all.

Remember the hand analogy in Chapter One? We can think of ourselves as separate, individual fingers or take our awareness up into the hand, where they are connected and further up to see that we are part of All That Is - connected to Source but also to each other, as part of the whole.

Even when we are physically alone, we need never be lonely. We only need to allow ourselves to be still, energetically open ourselves and yield to our Source of Unconditional Love. This energy is our spiritual home and can fill our being, our soul, nurturing, reassuring and connecting us at a deep level. (See Appendix,

Section C for the Source Connection Exercise on how to do this).

We can nurture ourselves anytime, by connecting to our Source of Unconditional Love – our spiritual home

Worrying About Problems in Life

It helps us if we 'see the big picture'. Problems which can seem unsurmountable can be transformed when we remember our eternal nature and, that the issues we are currently experiencing are actually a very small part of our totality.

There is a lovely story about a Chinese Farmer:

> *Once upon a time there was a Chinese farmer whose horse ran away. His neighbours came around to commiserate with him, saying how unfortunate it was that his horse had run away. The farmer said, 'Maybe it is, maybe it isn't.' The next day the horse came back bringing with him a number of wild horses and in the evening*

the neighbours came back and said, 'What marvellous news! What luck to have so many free horses!' The farmer again said, 'Maybe it is, maybe it isn't.'

The following day his son tried to break in one of the horses, was thrown and broke his leg. The neighbours again came and commiserated about the son's misfortune. The farmer responded, 'Maybe it is, maybe it isn't.' Soon afterwards, army officers came around to conscript his son into the army, but he was rejected because of his broken leg. Again, all the neighbours came around and said, 'Such great luck for your son to avoid conscription!' Again, the farmer said, 'Maybe it is, maybe it isn't.'

Our lives are complex. Something which appears on the surface to be 'bad' may turn out to be an important learning experience for us which we have chosen for our development, or it may be the repaying of karma which we agreed to do in this lifetime.

We are not victims of fate.

We have the power to transform our perception of reality through the power of our thoughts (Chapter Five). The realisation that we have the ability to create a better experience of our reality is extraordinarily powerful.

When we are faced with an apparently

unsurmountable problem, an extremely helpful thing to do is to offer the problem up to Source:

> Offering up my problems and worries to Source is something I find to be very effective. I remember one time, when I was leader of a team of volunteers in a hospice, there was a lady whose energy and behaviour were not in harmony with the other volunteers. She was giving her time freely and she was acting within the hospice guidelines, so it was difficult to pinpoint any particular issue to raise with her, except that her personality clashed with the others. Not an easy matter to have a conversation with a volunteer about! So, I just offered the situation to Source and a couple of days later, this lady phoned me to say that she was sorry to have to let us down, but she had just accepted an offer of full-time paid employment.

> I was able to thank her for her contribution to date and to wish her well in her new role.

> Problem solved for the benefit of all! Thank you.

Coping with Death and Dying

The notion of reincarnation (and the associated theory of karma) can be very comforting for many reasons:

- We do not just have this one life with all its problems. We can have other exciting lives and experiences if we choose to
- As we apparently incarnate within our soul group, we will have other lives with our loved ones, and we will be reunited with these souls when we die too
- Death is not the end for us. It is only the bridge into our next stage of being. We are energetic, eternal beings who are extensions of Source and who create and experience many lives
- A belief in reincarnation can help to explain our purpose in life – we may incarnate to experience, learn or teach
- Understanding things in this way can help us to be content with our lot in life –accepting that 'It's just the way it is' this time round. Some peoples' lives are plentiful and happy whilst others experience lack and sadness
- Reincarnation and karma can also explain the extremes and seeming unfairness we observe in the world

There are reports of their time between lives from clients under regression hypnosis, describing how we choose the basic outline of our physical existence to both learn and experience (Chapter Six). Love guides HOW we live our lives and through doing so influences WHAT happens in our lives.

Love guides HOW we live our lives and through doing so influences WHAT happens in our lives

Getting Sucked into the Drama of Others

So often people greet us with a story of what is going wrong for them, or the 'disasters' of other people they know. Initially we might have been feeling good but following the interaction we feel pulled down and lowly vibrational.

We feel as though we need to respond with sympathy or empathy, after all, that is what we have been taught is the caring way to be isn't it?

A response of **sympathy** actually comes from our personal expression of sadness or feeling of pity for the suffering of another. It is about *our own* feelings about the situation. We are not really 'present' for the other person if we respond with sympathy.

Communicating with **empathy** is how society expects us to respond and conveys that we deeply understand the emotions, thoughts or feelings of another from *their* point of view. People say such things as '*I feel your pain'*.

If we think about it, why on earth would we want to do that? Does it help the other person for us to be so affected by their story that it brings us down to the vibrational frequency of the storyteller? It certainly doesn't help them or us. Many carers and therapists work at the level of empathy, which can be very draining as they unknowingly bring their energetic frequency down to that of their client.

The best way is to communicate with **compassionate presence** which requires an ability to be compassionate while remaining quietly present for the other person, so you are not negatively affected by their mental or emotional state. Compassionate presence ensures that our energetic vibrations remain high, protected and grounded; it can help us to avoid becoming energetically depleted, whilst we offer support such as authentic listening.

> When I was director of a local charity, a participant in our programme said that she was unhappy about the attitude of one of the staff.
>
> I asked her to meet with me so that we could talk about her concerns.
>
> I could sense that she was very angry and when I looked at her energy field, there were spikes of energy being fired off into the atmosphere.
>
> Whilst I listened to her with compassionate presence, I asked Source for the energy of peace to go to her.
>
> After a few minutes, during which I offered to speak to the member of staff and she started

to calm down, she abruptly stopped speaking and said the unusual words, 'Thank you for your peace.'

I was amazed, not only had this lady felt the exact energy I had asked to be sent to her, but she also calmed down completely.

Her complaint was amicably resolved.

Listening is not the same as hearing. Peaceful, compassionate, deep listening means concentrating on what the other person is saying without the interruption of our own thoughts and feelings. It is about being fully present for the other person creating an atmosphere of tolerance and mutual caring. We need to listen not only to the words being spoken, but to how they are being spoken and the non-verbal messages sent with them. Deep, authentic listening takes place within (as opposed to between) two people and helps to neutralise feelings of anxiety and anger. It benefits the listener as well as the receiver through feelings of meaningful connection with each other.

Deep, authentic listening takes place *within* two people and allows feelings of meaningful connection

Feeling Powerless

When we feel powerless it is very helpful to remember that we are not just a physical form – we are a soul having an earthly journey in the current 'vehicle' of our body. We are energetic, eternal beings who are extensions of Source and who create and experience life (Chapter One). Since Source Energy is that of Unconditional Love, being consciously aware of the fact that we are extensions of that Love gives our existence the purpose of being in harmony with our true selves and manifesting Love in our lives.

Our creative minds are very powerful indeed (Chapter Five). Our positive thoughts and actions not only create a better reality for ourselves, but because we are energetic beings and connected to all, we also positively impact society and our world. So, no matter what the outward appearance and apparent inconsequence of our lives, if we manage our energetic vibrations through regular spiritual practise (Chapter Three) and radiate the highest vibration of unconditional love, we influence positively what happens in our own lives and the lives of others – A powerful thought!

Spending time with like-minded, positive people can also help. The combined energies of those with similar desires and aspirations can be very powerful.

Summary and Implications

Understanding and applying spiritual principles can be very helpful when dealing with inevitable challenges in life. It is not just theoretical knowledge (although this can help us understand what is happening and give us perspective), but it can practically help us and those around us.

The important thing is for us to take time to look after ourselves each day, to raise the frequency of our energetic vibrations and maintain this and so be in a better position to weather the storms of life. It empowers us to be the best that we can be, whatever our circumstances. It doesn't take long and we are worth it! We are magnificent, eternal, energetic beings, aspects of the unconditional love that is Source, living in an energetic world.

APPENDIX

Visualisation Exercises

A. Breathing in Peace' Meditation

This meditation is a simple and useful way to raise energetic vibrations by bringing peace into your being and to care for yourself.

Firstly, be aware of the ground beneath your feet. Feel the exchange of energy at that point, between your feet and the ground beneath. Feel the Earth supporting you....

Bring your attention to your breathing as you breathe in and out calmly through your nose... focusing mainly on the out-breath.

As you breathe in, know that you are breathing in peace and in the out-breath, feel that loving peace flow down into your body. So, breathing in peace and as you breathe out, this peace fills your being... In and within... Peace breathed in ....and within....

Gradually, as you absorb this feeling of peace, you know that it completely fills your being. You are peace...

This positive, peaceful energy expands beyond your physical body, about an arm's length in every direction, spreading peace around you, as a protective sphere. You are absorbed by this pure peaceful energy within and now radiating from you. You take time to appreciate this state of peace, which you have become...

Now bring your attention back to the soles of your feet and feel that connection with the Earth. Make sure that that you are grounded and know that your energies are now at an appropriate level for normal daily life. Open your eyes and give thanks for your transformed state of peace.

If you are feeling 'spaced out' after this visualisation, please see Section E about further grounding exercises, at the end of this appendix.

B. Sun Visualisation Exercise

This is a quick and easy way to raise your energetic vibrations and can be used regularly.

Take a few deep breaths. Focus your mind on the outbreath and as you do so allow calm to flow into your body......

Then breathe normally through your nose and feel your feet on the ground beneath you.

Now imagine that above you is a golden-coloured sphere of Light, like a huge sun. It is shining out rays of loving light towards you. It feels comfortably warm, welcoming and very safe.

Allow this sun to move down through the top of your head, to the level of your heart. Imagine the rays of light shining into every part of your body, so that you too glow with this light......

Feel the gentle, loving, Light energy clearing you, nourishing you, making you feel complete. You feel safe, empowered and very loved.

This Light keeps flowing into you so that the rays start to shine out of your body. The loving light is now filling you and shining outwards so that you are in the centre of a sphere of comforting, protecting light.

Enjoy this feeling. It is here for you any time you want it.

Now feel the ground beneath your feet and when you feel ready, open your eyes.

If you are feeling 'spaced out' after this visualisation, please see Section E about further grounding exercises, at the end of this appendix.

C. Source Connection Visualisation Exercise I

This is a very powerful visualisation exercise to raise your Energetic Vibration by connecting with the Source of Light, Love and Peace. It was channelled to us by Source and is the one which will most help you to raise your Energetic Vibration.

Firstly, whilst seated, close your eyes and take a few deep breaths. Focus your mind on the out-breath and as you do so allow calm to flow into your body......

Then breathe normally through your nose and ground yourself by focusing your mind on where the soles of your feet touch the ground. Feel the exchange of energy at that point, between your feet and the ground beneath. Feel the Earth supporting you....

Now take the focus of your attention into yourself, to the energy, the light that is the real you, your Life Force, your Soul. Even if you cannot 'see' this, just feel or know that this energy is there...

Now take your attention outwards until you see or sense, the Light and power of the Source of peace, love, healing and joy. Hold the intention of connecting that Light with your Life Force. As this loving energy flows towards you, allow this connection to happen. Feel it, see it, sense or just 'know' that this powerful Universal Energy is entering your Soul, strengthening it, enriching it, making you feel complete....

With every, gentle out-breath, allow this Light to expand so that it fills every cell of your body, nourishing, recharging, cleansing and healing....

Imagine the Light expanding further, beyond the boundaries of your body, about an arm's length in every direction - on either side, over your head and beneath your feet, in front and behind you. Imagine this powerful, peaceful, loving, energising Light continuing to connect with you, filling you, and expanding outwards until it is finally surrounding you, as a protective sphere. You are absorbed by this radiance, this power, this purest energy which fills you full of healing Light and surrounds you, comforts and protects you, cleanses, nourishes and recharges you...

Now bring your attention back to the soles of your feet and feel that connection with the Earth. Make sure that that you are grounded and know that your energies are now at an appropriate level for normal daily life. *You may find it helpful to visualise a flower closing at the top of your head........or put your hand on top of your head......*

When you feel ready, open your eyes and give thanks for this beautiful energy, given freely to you.

If you are feeling 'spaced out' after this visualisation, please see Section E about further grounding exercises, at the end of this appendix.

NOTE - If, in the above visualisation, you find it difficult to fill yourself with Source Energy, you might like to try the alternative method below:

Alternative Source Connection
Visualisation Exercise II

Firstly, whilst seated, close your eyes and take a few deep breaths. Focus your mind on the out-breath and as you do so allow calm to flow into your body......

Then breathe normally through your nose and ground yourself by focusing your mind on where the soles of your feet touch the ground. Feel the exchange of energy at that point, between your feet and the ground beneath. Feel the Earth supporting you....

Now take the focus of your attention into yourself, to the energy, the light that is the real you, your Life Force, your Soul. Even if you cannot 'see' this, just feel or know that this energy is there...

Now take your attention outwards until you see or sense, the Light and power of the Source of peace, love, healing and joy. Hold the intention of connecting that Light with your Life Force and, as this loving energy flows towards you, allow a beam of it to enter through the top of your head and go straight down into your feet, stopping at your soles. Then, at your own pace, let the energy begin to fill your body from your feet upwards.

With every gentle out-breath, allow this Light to continue expanding upwards from your feet, remembering to include your arms. Feel it, see it, sense or just 'know' that this powerful Universal Energy is entering your Soul, strengthening and enriching it.

At this point, when you are absolutely full, allow the beam of energy to continue flowing into you and, **whilst you remain full**, let the excess expand out beyond the boundaries of your body, about an arm's length in every direction - on either side, over your head and beneath your feet, in front and behind you. Imagine this powerful, peaceful, loving, energising Light continuing to connect with you, filling you, and expanding outwards until it is finally surrounding you, as a protective sphere.

You are absorbed by this radiance, this power, this purest energy which fills you full of healing Light and surrounds you, comforts and protects you, cleanses, nourishes and recharges you...

Now bring your attention back to the soles of your feet and feel that connection with the Earth. Make sure that that you are grounded and know that your energies are now at an appropriate level for normal daily life. *You may find it helpful to visualise a flower closing at the top of your head........or put your hand on top of your head.......*

When you feel ready, open your eyes and give thanks for this beautiful energy, given freely to you.

If you are feeling 'spaced out' after this visualisation, please see Section E about further grounding exercises, at the end of this appendix.

D. Bubbles of Light Protective Visualisation

This is a very useful exercise to protect your energies when there is a situation or person who tends to affect your energies adversely

Now, close your eyes and focus your mind on the out-breath. As you do so allow calm to flow into your body......

Be aware of the ground beneath your feet. Feel the exchange of energy at that point, between your feet and the ground beneath.

Now, visualise yourself surrounded by a pink bubble of light. It is the light of love and very powerful. It encloses you securely. You feel very safe. Even if you cannot see this bubble of protective, pink light, just know that it is there as your thoughts intend it to be.

Next, visualise the negative person or situation surrounded by a pink bubble of light. Know that this will separate you from that energy. Intend that positive energy can enter your bubble and lower vibrational energy is kept outside.

You are now protected, and your vibrations remain raised.

If you feel that this is appropriate, ask that loving energy (directly from Source, not from you) fills the second bubble knowing that this is transforming the energies within it.

Now bring your attention back to the soles of your feet and feel that connection with the Earth.

Open your eyes and give thanks that your energies remain positive.

If you are feeling 'spaced out' after this visualisation, please see Section E about further grounding exercises, at the end of this appendix.

E. Further Grounding Exercises

If after the visualisation exercise you are NOT FEELING FULLY GROUNDED or FEELING SPACED OUT, please do one or more of the following grounding exercises:

1. Sense the ground beneath your feet and feel the Earth supporting you. Feel the exchange of energy between the ground and the soles of your feet.

2. If you feel that you need further grounding, put a hand on the top of your head and then imagine golden roots growing from the soles of your feet into the centre of the Earth. These roots are grounding your energies to this physical reality. When you feel ready, you can remove your hand from your head and open your eyes.

3. Or if you are not able to visualise or sense energy, you can state your intention to be connected to the Earth and thank and know that this is the case.

BIBLIOGRAPHY

Chapter 1 – Who am I?

Brennan, B. A. *Hands of Light. A Guide to Healing Through the Human Energy Field.* New York. Bantam Books. 1988

Cheung, T. *The Afterlife in Real.* Simon and Schuster UK Ltd. 2013

Cohen, A. *A Course in Miracles Made Easy.* Hay House Inc. 2015

Hicks, E. & J. (The Teachings of Abraham). *Ask and It Is Given – Learning to Manifest Your Desires.* Hay House Inc. 2004

McTaggart, L. *The Field.* Element (Harper Collins Publishers Ltd), London, 2003

Moorjani, A. *Dying to be Me.* Hay House Inc. 2014

Olsen, J. and Nelson, L. *I knew their Hearts.* Cedar Fort Inc., 2012

Schucman, H. (Scribe) & Thetford, W. *A Course in Miracles.* (The Combined Volume, Third Edition) The Foundation for Inner Peace, Mill Valley, California. 2007

Smith, G. *Beyond Reasonable Doubt: The case for supernatural phenomena in the modern world.* Hodder and Stoughton Ltd, London. 2018

Watts, A. W. *The Essential Alan Watts.* Celestial Arts. 1995

Chapter 2 – The Purpose of Life

Cohen, A. *A Course in Miracles Made Easy.* Hay House Inc. 2015

Watts, A. W. *The Culture of Counter-Culture: Edited Transcripts (Love of Wisdom).* Tuttle Publishing. 1999

Chapter 3 - Positively Managing Our Personal Energy Field

Brennan, B. A. *Hands of Light. A Guide to Healing Through the Human Energy Field.* Bantam Books. New York. 1988

Dispenza, J. *Becoming Supernatural: How Common People are Doing the Uncommon.* Hay House Inc. New York. 2017

McTaggart, L. *The Field.* Element (Harper Collins Publishers Ltd), London, 2003

Chapter 4 - Our Reality

Cohen, A. *A Course in Miracles Made Easy.* Hay House Inc. 2015

Galfard, C. *The Universe in Your Hand. A journey through space, time and beyond.* Pan Macmillan, London. 2016

Greemblatt, M. *The Essential Teachings of Ramana Maharshi: A Visual Journey.* Inner Directions 2002

Henry R.C. The Mental Universe. *Nature 436:29,* July 2005

Hoffman, D. Conscious Realism and the Mind-Body Problem, *Mind & Matter* 2008 Vol. 6(1), pp. 87-121

Ideapod Academy. *35 of the most mind opening quotes from Alan Watts* - https://ideapod.com/25-mind-opening-quotes-alan-watts/ [Accessed 14-1-20]

Radin D. *Entangled Minds – Extrasensory Experiences in a Quantum Reality.* Paraview Pocket Books, New York, 2006

Samanta-Laughton, M. *Punk Science: Inside the Mind of God*. John Hunt Publishing Ltd, UK 2006

Schucman, H. (Scribe) & Thetford, W. *A Course in Miracles*. (The Combined Volume, Third Edition) The Foundation for Inner Peace, Mill Valley, California 2007

Sugano H, Uchida S, Kuramato I. A new approach to the studies of subtle energies' *Subtle Energies*.1994; 5(2): 602-607

Talbot M. *The Holographic Universe*. Harper Collins, London 1996

Skenderis K. *Study Reveals Substantial Evidence of Holographic Universe.* University of Southampton (2017) - https://www.southampton.ac.uk/news/2017/01/holographic-universe.page [Accessed 16-5-20]

Walia A. *'Consciousness Creates Reality' – Physicists admit the Universe is Immaterial, Mental and Spiritual* http://www.collective-evolution.com/2014/11/11/consciousness-creates-reality-physicists-admit-the-universe-is-immaterial-mental-spiritual/ [Accessed 16-5-20]

What the Bleep!?: Down the Rabbit Hole (2006) – This docudrama film illustrates the link between quantum mechanics, neurobiology, human consciousness and day-to-day reality.

Chapter 5 – Our Powerful, Creative Mind

Dispenza, J. *Becoming Supernatural: How Common People are Doing the Uncommon*. Hay House Inc. New York. 2017

Hicks, E. & J. (The Teachings of Abraham). *Ask and It Is Given – Learning to Manifest Your Desires*. Hay House Inc. 2004

Lipton, B.H. *The Biology of Belief – Unleashing the power of Consciousness, Matter and Miracles*. Hay House Inc., New York, 2015

Bruce Lipton - *Biology of Belief - Part 1/2* London Real: https://www.youtube.com/watch?v=GCG1zj3mxOw [Accessed 16-5-20]

King, Vex. *Good Vibes, Good Life. How self-love is the key to unlocking your greatness.* Hay House, London. 2018

Seligman, M. E., Steen, T. A., Park, N., & Peterson, C. Positive psychology progress: empirical validation of interventions. *American Psychologist*, 2005. *60* (5), 410

Chapter 6 – We Choose this Life!

Cannon, D. Dolores Cannon on Reincarnation: http://www.dolorescannon.com/blog/dolores-cannon-reincarnation [Accessed 22-8-19]

Newton, M. *Journey of Souls: Case Studies of Life between Lives.* Llewellyn Publications 1996

Weiss, B. *Many Lives, Many Masters.* Grand Central Publishing, New York 1996

Chapter 7 – More About Looking After Ourselves - Because it is so important!

Centers for Disease Control and Prevention. *Coping with Stress* - http://www.cdc.gov/violenceprevention/pub/coping with stress tips.html [Accessed 18-1-20]

HelpGuide. *Healthy Eating* - https://www.helpguide.org/articles/healthy-eating/healthy-eating.htm [Accessed 18-1-20]

Tolle, E. *The Power of Now. A Guide to Spiritual Enlightenment.* New World Library 1999

Walker, M. *Why We Sleep: The New Science of Sleep and Dreams.* Penguin 2018

Chapter 8 – Forgiveness = Spiritual Growth

Dupree, U. E. Ho'oponopno – *The Hawaiian Forgiveness Ritual as The Key to Your Life's Fulfilment*. Earthdancer Books 2012

Hay, Louise *You can Heal Your Life.* Hay House 2005

LaBianca, J. *14 Proven Steps to Truly Forgive Anyone for Anything*. https://www.rd.com/advice/relationships/best-way-to-forgive/ [Accessed 17-5-20]

Martin, W. *Four Steps to Forgiveness. A powerful way to freedom, happiness and success.* Findhorn Press 2014

Schucman, H. (Scribe) & Thetford, W. *A Course in Miracles.* (The Combined Volume, Third Edition) The Foundation for Inner Peace, Mill Valley, California 2007

Whyte, D. *Consolations – The Solace, Nourishment and Underlying Meaning of Everyday Words.* Many Rivers Press. Langley, Washington 2015

Chapter 9 – Empaths, Sensitives and Intuition

Orloff, J. *The Empath's Survival Guide: Life Strategies for Sensitive People.* True Sounds. 2018

Chapter 10 – Practically Applying Spiritual Principles to Life's Challenges

Hibbert, Noor. *Just F*cking Do It! Stop Playing Small. Transform your Life*. John Murray Learning. 2019

AUTHOR BIOGRAPHY

Su Mason Ph.D. B.Nurs. and Kathleen Judd both regard themselves as souls on an earthly journey. They are founding Directors of *Omnes Healing Limited* (www.omneshealing.com), a not-for-profit healing organisation which trains students in Source Attunement Healing (to UK Healers and The Confederation of Healing Organisations standards), and a healer membership organisation that provides energy rebalancing for the public.

They both devote their time to the practise and teaching of healing/energy rebalancing and managing *Omnes Healing.* Between them they have accumulated over seventy years of healing experience, teaching, channelling wisdom and guidance from Source and spiritual/personal development. Their specialist interests are clearing lower vibrational energies from people and spaces and soul fragmentation retrieval.

Su has a background as a Senior Nursing Sister of a regional, children's Burns Unit and was Joint Head of the Clinical Trials Research Unit at the University of

Leeds, UK, from 1998 to 2002. She now lives and works approximately half the year in Tobago, West Indies.

Kathleen has had a varied professional career. With approximately forty years' experience as a healer, her life is now dedicated to private practise and voluntary healing work. She is also an animal communicator.

ENDNOTES

1   Please note that the contents of this book are not intended to replace medical treatment or recognised therapy for any physical or mental health problems.

2   Channelled information is essentially done by a person connecting to the Highest Source for guidance and being aware of the wisdom received. Everyone is able to do this as we are all of Source, however, most people are unaware of this ability and so do not exercise it.

3   Cheung (2013) writes that in an empathetic near-death experience, people who are present when someone is dying can have an out-of-body experience themselves and then, afterwards they find themselves back in their body but are spiritually transformed.

4   It is worth noting that a person with high energetic vibrations does not necessarily mean someone with high physical energy. We are talking about the quality of the vibrations. High vibrational frequency can mean stillness and the person is more likely to radiate qualities such as peace, calmness, deep wisdom and contentment.

5   If you prefer to have someone guiding you through the exercises when you practise them, these energy vibration-raising exercises are on the '*Energeased*' CD which is available on www.omneshealing.com (and also as a download.)

6   This information about Karma and Reincarnation is based on current theories and understandings and is intended

only to define and explain their respective meanings. This material is not intended to try to either prove or disprove the existence of these concepts or suggest that any person is to blame in some way for their own, or someone else's, ill health or lack of abundance.